culture matters

culture matters

A CALL FOR CONSENSUS ON CHRISTIAN CULTURAL ENGAGEMENT

t. m. moore

BrazosPress
Grand Rapids, Michigan

© 2007 by T. M. Moore

Published by Brazos Press
a division of Baker Publishing Group
P.O. Box 6287, Grand Rapids, MI 49516-6287
www.brazospress.com

Printed in the United States of America

Library of Congress Cataloging-in-Publication Data
Moore, T. M. (Terry Michael), 1949–
    Culture matters : a call for consensus on Christian cultural engagement /
T. M. Moore.
        p.   cm.
    Includes bibliographical references.
    ISBN 10: 1-58743-187-4 (pbk.)
    ISBN 978-1-58743-187-6 (pbk.)
    1. Christianity and culture. I. Title.
BR115.C8M65   2007
261—dc22   2007009050

Contents

117295

Foreword

EVEN IF FISH can think, they likely give little thought to the water in which they swim. Similarly, *culture* is the taken-for-granted air of ideas, habits, hopes, and fears that we breathe every day. Unlike fish, however, we human beings can and should think about it, and we can and should do something about it.

In this masterful little book, T. M. Moore sketches the ways in which Christians engage, resist, escape from, and try to change the culture in which they live. There is no one right way—either in the past or the present—for Christians to respond to the culture of which they are part. I appreciate his generous words on the ways in which we try to do it in *First Things*. This book lifts up the examples of others who exemplify other ways of doing it. There is, for example, the Dutch Calvinist Abraham Kuyper and my friend Charles Colson. Especially insightful is the author's treatment of the poet Czeslaw Milosz.

For all our numbers and positions of influence, we Christians in America have a lot to learn about engaging the culture. Some have concentrated on political influence, and that is not unimportant. But politics is, I believe, in largest part a function of culture; at the heart of culture is morality; and at the heart of morality are the commanding truths usually associated with religion. For Christians, the commanding truth of commanding truths is that Jesus Christ is Lord. That the lordship of Christ is already assured in his cross, and resurrection is the source of Christian confidence in engaging the culture, as in everything else we do.

There are today many people involved in "Christian music," "Christian publishing," "Christian poetry," and "Christian arts." These efforts have created a huge industry in "Christian culture." This culture may be viewed as an alternative culture to the culture that dominates American life. Too often, however, it is no more than a subculture. Whether in literature, music, or the arts, it is, so to speak, preaching to the choir. Of course, the choir, too, needs preaching, but T. M. Moore urges us to expand our horizons.

Abraham Kuyper employs the idea of "spheres of sovereignty." There are certain human activities—familial, economic, political, literary, artistic—that have their own integrity, and that integrity must be respected. Such activities have their own history and criteria of excellence. Christians should be shaping that history and exemplifying that excellence. To be sure, we will often meet with resistance, just as Jesus promised his disciples that they would. There are many who control "the commanding heights of culture" (the phrase is from Karl Marx) who view anything Christian as second-rate, sectarian, and an instance of special pleading.

Too many Christians have internalized that view promoted by the cultured despisers of Christianity. They have resigned themselves to life in the Christian subculture, and are pitiably pleased when they receive a morsel of praise falling from the table of those on the commanding heights. Other Christians are pitiably pleased when they are given a place at the table "on good behavior"—meaning that they promise not to be too Christian.

T. M. Moore persuasively explains why we cannot be satisfied with those arrangements of cultural affairs. Also in the spheres of culture, Christians are called to the hard discipline of proposing and demonstrating a more excellent way. Cultural recognition is not to be demanded but earned.

In this connection and many others, we recall the words of St. Paul at the end of the twelfth chapter of First Corinthians. The Christians in Corinth, like Christians of our time, were fractious, quarrelsome, and bringing the name of Christ into ill repute. After addressing their many problems, Paul says, "Let me show you a more excellent way." That way is the way of love confidently grounded in the victory of Christ.

The book you have in hand is an invitation to a more excellent way. It is an invitation that should not be declined.

Richard John Neuhaus
Editor in Chief, *First Things*

Acknowledgments

I AM GRATEFUL TO Rodney Clapp and the staff at Brazos Press for taking this project under their wings. I also wish to express my gratitude to Richard John Neuhaus, Phil Keaggy, and Chuck Colson for their contributions to this volume, and especially to my wife, Susie, for her ever-valuable editorial assistance.

Introduction

CULTURE PLAYS A powerful role in human life. We cannot live without it, yet we are often confused about how to regard it, or what to do with it. The artifacts, institutions, and conventions with which we surround ourselves—our culture—help us to define, sustain, and enrich our lives and experience. The forms of culture are many and varied: they can be as exotic and complex as an opera or as commonplace and everyday as a conversation across the back fence. They include the books and magazines we read, the decor with which we adorn our homes, and our tastes in fashion and music. Culture can be as interesting as the current best seller or as irritating as the music that intrudes on our meal at a restaurant.

Aspects of culture disturb us, or even threaten our well-being. Culture influences the way we view the world and the use we make of it. It shapes our outlook and affections, facilitates our work, conveys our understanding and convictions, variously delights and edifies or troubles and dismays us, and constitutes part of the legacy we will leave for future generations. Culture lets us make a statement about who we are and what matters to us. As a result, culture often divides us; but it can also serve as a meeting ground for common concerns. The ongoing "culture wars" remind us that, as Christians, we cannot afford the luxury of a studied indifference with respect to so potent a subject. Culture matters, and our approach to it must be as informed and consistent as possible.

The Christian community today is divided about culture matters as they relate to the life of faith. No consensus exists among the followers of Christ concerning how to approach and make use of the artifacts, institutions, and conventions of culture in a decidedly *Christian* manner, and this in spite of the fact that we are called to do all things unto the glory of God (1 Cor. 10:31). Instead, Christians are divided among themselves about culture matters, and thus present no united front for responding to the contemporary cultural situation with viable Christian alternatives. A brief survey of the state of Christian approaches to culture matters will be helpful in demonstrating the need for working toward a consensus in this important area.

Christian Approaches to Culture

We may identify at least six different contemporary Christian approaches to culture matters. The first we may call *cultural indifference*. Perhaps the vast majority of contemporary Christians hardly give culture a second thought, at least as it relates to their faith in Christ. It's not that they're not engaged in culture; they just don't think about their involvement all that much, at least not from the perspective of their Christian beliefs. They have simply absorbed the tastes, habits, manners, and cultural preferences of their environment throughout the course of their lives. For the most part, their cultural practices reflect the standards and preferences of the people and the environment around them. While most Christians will not condone the more extreme expressions of sensuality, violence, or relativism in the culture at large, still, the culture to which they incline—their tastes in fashion and entertainment, their political inclinations, how they spend their time and money, their topics of conversation—differs but little from that of their non-Christian friends and associates.

A second way our division over culture matters is manifest is in what we might call *cultural aversion*. For some, especially ultraconservative Christians, culture is a blight to be avoided, an evil in which we must not participate. Unlike those in the first category, who scarcely think about culture in the light of their Christian convictions, believers in this group are highly sensitive to the ways contemporary culture threatens their beliefs, morals, and institutions. Culture is of this world, they insist, and anything of this world has the potential to undermine Christian faith. The best approach to culture, therefore, is just to avoid it, keep away from, lest it contaminate your faith. The only legitimate cultural activities are those that relate to the necessities of survival and the mission of the gospel, or those that can be safely entered into within the confines of family and the community of faith.

A third expression of cultural division on the part of Christians we might call *cultural trivialization.* Christians who practice this approach want a distinctively Christian cultural expression, but they tend to limit that to popular forms and artifacts, the bulk of which partake of a tiresome sameness. This category includes much of Christian pop music as well as the "bookstore culture"—plaques and posters, knick-knacks and gewgaws, jewelry and junk, T-shirts and trivia—that keeps most Christian bookstores afloat. One group of the forms of culture characteristic of this category typically includes varieties of folk art or personal couture adorned with Bible verses, familiar Christian symbols, cutesy Bible characters, and the ever-increasing variety of Christian-theme prints. In the area of contemporary music, forms popular in the secular world are adapted for Christian audiences, with themes and lyrics reflecting narrowly spiritual concerns. Culture is trivialized in this approach in two ways: (1) by narrowing the range of cultural forms—music, crafts, and personal accoutrements—and (2) by the narrowly spiritual themes addressed or represented by those forms. The effect of such trivialization of culture is to limit the significance of culture matters to the merely personal and narrowly pious.

A fourth evidence of division among Christians over matters of culture we might call *cultural accommodation.* Many Christians seem to regard it as the duty of the faithful to make room in their beliefs and lifestyles for whatever new expressions of culture may appear. These members of the community of faith espouse a pluralistic and nonjudgmental approach to culture, a kind of "live-and-let-live" approach to matters of taste, preference, and practice in the cultural arena. Cultural preference is regarded as a matter of strictly personal choice, qualified by the determination to extend this privilege to all, while seeking to preserve the dignity and well-being of others. Unlike the members of the first category, who think very little about culture matters, and thus tend to reflect the cultural preferences and practices of the moment, those who hold to some form of cultural accommodation mirror the culture of the day out of a self-conscious sense of Christian conviction.

A fifth evidence of division over culture matters can be seen among members of the Christian community who practice what we might call *cultural separation*. Proponents of this approach tend to hold to a broad view of culture, but they work the hardest in culture matters in the area of promoting and constructing Christian alternatives to the existing culture, alternatives that are primarily for their own use and that of their Christian families, friends, and neighbors. They adopt forms of alternative schooling to keep their children free from the influences of secularism, decorate their homes and persons with decidedly Christian cultural artifacts, and create Christian sports leagues and other kinds of associations for recreation and ministry within the safe confines of the believing community. They publish and use a wide variety of Christian "Yellow Pages" in an effort to ensure that their toilets and sinks will be kept clear by only Christian plumbers. They listen to Christian radio, watch Christian television, and even go to Christian nightclubs when they can find one. Their cultural interests are broader than the *culture trivializers* and more clearly Christian than the *accommodationists*, but they have little influence in culture matters beyond their own narrowly Christian spheres. Culture is a way of protecting themselves and their families from the harmful effects of contemporary culture by providing as wide an array of cultural alternatives as possible within the safe confines of the believing community.

A final contemporary Christian approach to culture we might refer to as *culture triumphalism*. These Christians expect too much of culture; they believe that by voting for the right candidates, changing laws, securing the right judges, suppressing this aspect of culture while promoting that, and seeking to impose their own cultural preferences and practices on others through legislative, judicial, and ecclesiastical processes they will best be able to advance the kingdom of God. Such aspiration seeks a society characterized by righteousness, peace, and joy *though renewed culture*, rather than by the Spirit of God, as Paul directs (Rom. 14:17). While we may admire the zeal for culture expressed in this approach, and want to gloat with the proponents of this view over every indication of some victory (however small), still, this approach to culture matters demands more than culture can perform; and it tends to alienate people from all places on the cultural spectrum by what often appear to be exclusivist, outrageous, and unrealizable demands.

No one adheres to any of these six models as the exclusive or even self-conscious approach to culture matters. In fact, each of us may find aspects of these Christian approaches to culture in our own practice. We are all somewhat inattentive to or indifferent toward the way we use culture, in that we do not give consistently Christian thought to all the many forms and aspects of culture in which we engage. We feel aversion to forms of culture that offend Christian sensibilities. We all enjoy a bit of trivialized Christian culture, and we are happy to accommodate aspects of contemporary non-Christian forms of culture that please us or satisfy some need. We all practice a kind of cultural separationism at times—indulging our distinctly Christian interests with Christian friends in acceptable Christian contexts and ways—just as we all relish a little cultural triumphalism when "our side" makes a point or appears to gain ground against competing views. Our confusion over culture matters could hardly be more evident.

Seeking Consensus on Culture

It is clear from these different approaches to culture matters that little in the way of a vital consensus on the use of culture exists among the members of the community of Christian faith. While these approaches may overlap at various points, and among individual believers, none of them has, to this point, provided a viable, consensual approach to culture matters that can unite Christians in common cultural endeavor and provide us a platform for pursuing the progress of Christ's kingdom in all areas of life. Thus, a number of important questions remain to be answered: Does it matter how we approach culture matters? If so, why? How shall we regard culture, and to what ends shall we make and use it? How does culture fit in with the mission of the church and the calling to make disciples? Where can we look for models to guide us in cultural endeavors? Is it possible to achieve even the beginnings of a Christian consensus on culture?

It can be helpful, in seeking to discover some aspects of a common approach to culture matters, to look to our Christian past, as well as to the scriptures and the example of Christian contemporaries. Here we can examine the thinking and practice of our predecessors and friends in the faith as they have considered and interacted with the culture of their day in the light of God's Word and expressed their views and practices of culture matters. This book will examine

Christian approaches to culture from five periods of church history, looking at four individuals and one school of practitioners whose approaches and practices can help us to discern some guidelines for a Christian consensus on culture matters for our own day. In addition, we shall consider the teaching of scripture on culture matters as well as the work of certain of our contemporaries in this arena.

We look first at Augustine. In his great work *City of God*, we find a devastating critique of the pagan culture of his day and are urged to see that all our work in the area of culture requires critical reflection and interaction with the artifacts, institutions, and conventions of the world in which we live. We cannot simply ignore contemporary culture; nor should we adopt an uncritical approach to it, particularly when, in many ways, contemporary culture seems bent on marginalizing or neutralizing the faith. Augustine teaches us that we must have a sound approach in our critique of culture, one that is grounded both in the Word of God and the demands of consistent thinking and living. In the widely read Christian monthly *First Things*, we find a salutary example of a contemporary Christian approach to the critique of culture, one that follows the guidelines of Augustine in ways from which we may benefit in our understanding of and approach to the culture of our day.

In chapter 2 we will examine the cultural achievement of the Celtic Christian period in the visual arts. Artists of this period show us that, while the culture around us may be inherently evil or even openly hostile to our biblical worldview, it nevertheless contains forms, themes, and genre from which we may be able to forge entirely new cultural expressions, distinctly Christian in nature. In one sense, all culture is a gift from God. The challenge to us is in learning how to take what is good in contemporary culture, reclaim and retool it, and put it to work in a Christian framework for the sake of forging new culture. Guitarist and composer Phil Keaggy demonstrates in his own work in culture many of the principles pioneered by our Celtic Christian forebears; his example can encourage us as we take up the work of forging new culture in an age of cultural confusion and decline.

Obviously, we will have a good deal of study, reflecting, and learning to do as we take up the work of critiquing culture and forging new culture that is distinctively Christian in its various expressions. Conscientious Christian engagement with culture matters requires a concerted work of Christian education. Much of this will involve us in the use of inherited cultural forms; at the same time, it will require that we employ those forms in a broadened curriculum and in innovative educational programs, and according to a distinctly Christian philosophy of instruction. In chapter 3 we will examine the work of the great sixteenth-century reformer John Calvin, as we consider what may be required of us educationally in preparing for a renewed consensus on culture matters. Further, by examining the Centurions training program of the BreakPoint division of Prison Fellowship Ministries, we will discover some creative and effective ways of beginning to promote a more biblical consensus on culture matters throughout the church.

As we prepare to take up the work of Christ's kingdom through the various agencies and aspects of culture, we will be looking for some general principles around which wide agreement can be reached, and that can guide us in all our work in culture. Often, we may discover those principles embodied in the work of some individual from the Christian past, from whom we may learn how to take up the challenge of culture matters in our day. In chapter 4 we will look at the cultural work and writings of Abraham Kuyper, the great nineteenth-century Dutch theologian, educator, journalist, and statesman. Kuyper reflected long and hard on culture matters and has left a legacy of valuable writings to help us in discovering general principles for achieving a Christian consensus on them. In our day Charles Colson, founder of Prison Fellowship Ministries, has been used of God to open many opportunities for Christians to express their kingdom convictions in a wide range of cultural arenas. We shall talk with him about his own involvement in culture matters. His example, like that of Abraham Kuyper, can inspire and guide us as we begin the basis of a Christian consensus in culture matters to seek the kingdom of God across a broad spectrum.

One of the most important uses to which culture can be put is in interpreting the times in which we live and setting forth the distinctive aspects of a Christian worldview as an alternative to the various life systems of unbelief. Culture can play a powerful prophetic role in the work of Christ's kingdom, both by exposing the folly of contemporary life and by pointing the way to renewal. The arts especially can be a potent force in this endeavor, for they appeal not only to Christians but to the wider public as well. In chapter 5 we will examine the poetic views and work of Nobel prizewinner Czeslaw Milosz, the twentieth century's most theological poet, and one of its most highly regarded. From his example we will identify guidelines for encouraging a more consistent and determined effort at setting forth the biblical worldview through our involvement in culture matters in an age straddling the cusp of the modernist/postmodernist divide. In the world of Christian pop culture, guitarist and composer David Wilcox stands as a kind of "prophet-under-the-radar" to lead us in examining our own lives in culture, and to point the way to more consistent expressions of our Christian faith.

Each chapter includes questions for study or discussion to help in personalizing the observations and lessons from each period and example. Our final chapter brings together the lessons learned from each of the preceding chapters, as we consider some parameters of a Christian consensus on culture matters and suggest ways that individual believers and their communities can begin to contribute to that consensus.

Culture Matters

Indeed, culture matters. As Christians we must discover ways of joining together to reconcile this important, inescapable aspect of our experience to God, so that we can fulfill the obligation incumbent on all the followers of Christ of doing everything—including our work in culture—as part of our quest for the kingdom of God and the glory of his name (Matt. 6:33). My hope for this book is that it will spark discussion among Christians in all the arenas of the life of faith, and from a broad range of ecclesiastical, theological, and cultural perspectives, leading to better understanding and clearer and more widespread agreement on culture matters within the body of Christ.

Only as we join together to talk, pray, debate, study, and labor can we ever hope to achieve a meaningful consensus on culture matters, one that can enable us to demonstrate together the power of the gospel to make all things new, including every aspect of culture. With our predecessors and contemporaries as guides, the Word of God as our touchstone, and the kingdom of God our common pursuit, we may yet find a way to tell the old, old story of Jesus and his love with one compelling voice, through all the various forms and expressions of culture.

T. M. Moore
Concord, Tennessee
Winter 2006

Culture Matters

Augustine and the Critique of Contemporary Culture

Radical Christians will be iconoclasts intent on bringing down the secular towers of Babel, which often wear a religious label. Such Christians will be considered spiritual and even social revolutionaries, for they will be conspicuous in their refusal to pay obeisance to the false gods that enthrall a secular culture.

Donald Bloesch

Jesus answered them, "I did one deed, and you all marvel at it. Moses gave you circumcision (not that it is from Moses, but from the fathers), and you circumcise a man on the Sabbath. If on the Sabbath a man receives circumcision, so that the law of Moses may not be broken, are you angry with me because on the Sabbath I made a man's whole body well? Do not judge by appearances, but judge with right judgment."

John 7:21–24[1]

T HE RELIGIOUS AND political leaders of Jesus's day joined forces to oppose him, in no small part because they perceived him to be a threat to their social and cultural privileges. They saw his claims, works, and teachings as offering a stinging critique of the status quo and feared that, unless he were stopped, this radical prophet might bring about dramatic changes in the social order (cf. John 12:45–48; 19:12–16). As it turned out, they were correct, as the nervous citizens of Thessalonica would later attest (Acts 17:1–9).

While it was not the mission of Jesus to serve as a critic of culture, the mission on which he *was* sent inevitably found him engaging in just such activity. In order to find the lost and bring them into the light of truth, so that they might be saved, Jesus often found it necessary to expose the darkness—the mistaken notions and the lies, half-truths, and outright deceptions—of the prevailing order. He did not hesitate to confront the various aspects of first-century Hebrew/Roman culture when his mission required him to do so. Indeed, he often went to dramatic lengths to ensure that his "critique" of the culture of his day received widespread attention, as when he violently disrupted the illicit commerce in the temple, or when he boldly confronted the mistaken opinions and practices of the theologians of his day, in full view of the astonished public.

But Jesus's critique of contemporary culture was not entirely negative. He drew upon aspects of the culture of his day to help further his mission, employing various artifacts (coins, clothing, implements, tools), conventions (language, holy days, instructional methods), and institutions (kingdoms, marriage, civil and religious authority structures) as illustrations or vehicles through which to assert his unique calling and pursue the unfolding of the kingdom of God. Some aspects of the culture of his day Jesus regarded as corrupt and corrupting, and he opposed them for the sake of the greater good of the kingdom of God. Other aspects of his culture he considered to be legitimate, even necessary, to the work of bringing that kingdom to expression. Those he freely used and recommended to his followers.

For Jesus, culture was inevitable and inescapable, just as it is for all of us. Culture consists of the artifacts, institutions, and conventions by which people define, sustain, and enrich their lives. Human beings are creatures of culture; we require it for our very existence and could not avoid or escape it even if we tried. Culture is inevitable, even essential. But not all culture is edifying, and this is especially so when our objective in life is the realization of the kingdom of righteousness, peace, and joy in the Holy Spirit (Matt. 6:33; Rom. 14:17). Some aspects of culture will present obstacles to the pursuit of the Kingdom of God, while other aspects can be useful in expressing and furthering that enterprise. The challenge to those called to seek first the kingdom of God and his righteousness is to be able to determine which is which, and to evaluate and employ culture in ways consistent with our callings as followers of the Lord.

To this end we must learn, as Jesus taught, to look beyond the superficial aspects of culture to the deeper levels of what makes culture what it is. We must be able to examine the culture of our day with a critical eye, and to judge with righteous judgment how we are to respond to, engage with, employ, and improve the culture in which we live. And this would seem to be especially true when proponents of any particular culture seek to employ or defend it against the interests of the kingdom of God.[2]

The Sack of Rome and the Search for a Scapegoat

In AD 410 the Western world was rocked to its foundations by the news that the barbarians under Alaric had entered and sacked Rome, the Eternal City and capital of the civilized world. While Rome had long since ceased to be the center of the empire, the effect of this event throughout the Roman world was, as Henry Chadwick observed, "numbing."[3] People wanted to know why. What was the cause of this disaster? How could this have happened? Pagan refugees who had escaped the destruction of the city and were arriving in North Africa offered their own explanations: the ancient gods of Rome had wrought this havoc because the people had abandoned them for the religion of Christianity. They threw the gauntlet of blame for the sack of Rome at the feet of the church. If only the good people of Rome had clung to their ancient faith and culture, this tragedy would not have occurred.

These charges soon came to the attention of the Bishop of Hippo, Augustine, and he determined that this challenge must not go unanswered. Over the next thirteen years he issued, in installments, a devastating broadside against the claims of the apologists of Roman culture. In *City of God* we may discern the outlines of one of the first great Christian critiques of pagan culture.[4] His work can serve as a guideline for us in keeping watch on the culture of our own day.[5]

The charges

The pagan refugees who began arriving in Hippo in 411 laid two primary charges at the feet of the Christians. First, they insisted that Rome had fallen into barbarian hands because the people of

Rome had forsaken the ancient cult of Roman gods for the practice of Christianity. Rome had perished because "it had lost the gods as guardians."[6] They attempted to buttress this charge by trumpeting the outrages perpetrated against many Christians during the days of Rome's violation by the barbarians, including rape, dispossession, and their dead being left unburied. The violence of the pagan hordes against ordinary Christians proved to these disgruntled Romans that the religion of Christ was the focus of the gods' wrath and the cause of Rome's tragedy. The gods, offended at having been neglected for so long, had finally visited judgment against their ancient home. The implicit claim accompanying this charge was that the gods of ancient Rome, and all the culture associated with them, were more to be preferred than that cult and culture which had arisen throughout the world since the days of Constantine and Theodosius.

Second, those who faulted Christianity for the fall of Rome charged that, at any rate, Rome had been better off—more noble, just, and decent—under the ancient gods than under the rule of Christ.[7] Christianity had in fact been the cause of Rome's degradation and fall. Roman religion had produced, if not a golden age, at least a time of peace, universal happiness, and exemplary civic morality. The survivors of Rome's sack claimed that, back when the gods were honored, people did not have to live in fear of barbarian hordes. They enjoyed honest work and abundant diversions. Civility prevailed throughout the world under the impetus of Roman law and religion. The pagan refugees from Rome ranted against Christianity, lamenting that, under that faith, Rome had "declined from good by degrees, and from an honest and honourable state . . . into the greatest dishonesty and dishonour possible."[8]

These two charges, accompanied by a variety of claims and evidences, could not go unanswered. In responding, Augustine mounted his great Christian apologetic against a hostile culture and pointed the way for us to judge with righteous judgment as we keep watch on the culture of our own day.

City of God: Outlines of a response

These charges by Christianity's pagan detractors provided the focus for Augustine's massive defense of the Christian worldview. We may identify seven aspects of his response to Christianity's detractors in City of God that can guide us in taking up the task of cultural criticism in our own day. I shall summarize these here and then develop them somewhat more fully in the section that follows.

First, Augustine's critique of pagan culture was *timely*. He recognized the seriousness of the charges and realized that, while they may not agree with the pagan claims, many Christians were wondering the same thing: why had Rome come to judgment? And why were Christians suffering along with everyone else? The welfare of his flock demanded that Augustine lose no time in answering the church's questions as well as her critics.

Second, Augustine was *principled* in his critique. This is not to say that he did not throw in the occasional barb or knock over a straw man here or there. For the most part, however, the great bishop was concerned to focus on the charges of Christianity's detractors and to evaluate the soundness of those charges in the light of the facts.

Third, Augustine's critique was *fair*. Whenever he could say something positive about Roman culture, he did not hesitate to do so. He showed respect where it was due and did not try to reinterpret facts or events in a way biased to support his case. Further, he let the pagan philosophers and theologians speak for themselves and evaluated them according to their own words.

Fourth, his response to the church's critics was *reasoned*. Augustine held his detractors to their charges and evaluated the extent to which the claims supporting these charges were consistent, coherent, and congruent with reality. He forced the critics of Christianity, as well as his believing readers, to examine the pagan claims in the light of Roman history and their own experience.

Fifth, Augustine did not hesitate to take a *theological* approach to responding to his critics. In his response he examined underlying theological issues, exposing the vapidity of the pagan charges and asserting the strength and integrity of the Christian faith. He assumed that theological issues were at the root of this criticism, and he addressed them boldly and forcefully.

Sixth, his critique was *evangelical*. As often as it fit the point he was making, Augustine preached the gospel to his critics and reminded his Christian readers of the glory that was theirs in Christ. Further, he elaborated a defense of Christianity from a biblical and theological perspective, showing how all the ancient scriptures point to Jesus as the promised Messiah.

Finally, Augustine's approach to Christianity's detractors was *visionary*. He was not content merely to refute the charges of his critics. Instead, he went on to paint a majestic landscape of the unfolding kingdom of Christ and the hope of eternal glory and bliss. Thus, he hoped to encourage Christian readers to cling to their hope in Christ, and to silence the pagan critics of the faith.

We turn now to examine more carefully these different aspects of Augustine's critique of the pagan Roman culture of his day.

Augustine's Critique of Culture

I want to sample each of these aspects of Augustine's critique of Roman culture, illustrating from *City of God* an approach to judging with righteous judgment that can serve us today as we seek a Christian consensus on culture matters.[9] Then, in the final section of this chapter, we shall consider a contemporary model of an "Augustinian" critique of culture that can serve us further in learning how to practice this important discipline in our day.

A timely critique

The charges laid at the feet of the Christian faith by the pagan refugees from Rome were very serious. For many who yet hankered for the old ways against the growing power of the church, the pagan explanation may have been persuasive. Even the followers of Christ were asking questions about why Rome had fallen, and why their fellow believers had been subjected to the kinds of outrages that were being reported. Augustine must have felt that there was a danger of an incipient movement of pagan revivalism, such as had briefly flourished under Julian a generation before, taking root on his watch in his own district. He needed to deflate the pagan boasts about the superiority of the ancient gods; but he also needed to provide a reasonable explanation for the suffering of the followers of Christ. He decided to begin with the latter, and to be brief about it, before offering an introductory, sweeping repudiation of the pagan charges in Books I through IV (issued between AD 413 and 415[10]).

Augustine took the occasion of the suffering of believers in Rome to warn his readers against relaxing their confidence in Christ. They must not make the mistake of thinking their detractors' explanation for the suffering of the Roman Christians was the only or best one. After a brief opening flourish against the detractors themselves, Augustine turned to the issue of the suffering of believers. He argued that God sometimes allows such suffering in order to purify and strengthen his church. Augustine wrote that, while Christians have been separated from the company of the wicked, "yet they should not hold themselves so purely separate from all faults, that they should think themselves too good to suffer a temporal correction for divers faults that might be found in their conversations."[11] Such corrections must come from time to time, since the saints in this life are not yet perfect, and are frequently influenced by the wickedness around them to indulge too much in the things of "this transitory life."[12] The believer is called to judge with righteous judgment the wicked acts and inclinations of the pagan world, which he "should contemn, that the other by him being corrected and amended might attain the life eternal."[13] When believers begin to relax vigilance in discipline and ministry—when their critical faculties grow lax and they leave off speaking prophetically to their contemporaries—God knows how to correct them. At the same time, Augustine sought to protect the honor of those who had suffered rape, assuring his readers that those who had been thus violated were not themselves guilty of sin in such cases.[14] The placement and brevity of this section of Book I seem intended as an admonition to any Christian readers who might have been receiving the pagan argument favorably: they must not themselves fall into the same "disordered life"[15] that may have been the occasion of God's discipline on their brethren to the north. Rather than think of relaxing their faith and returning to the gods of Rome, they must renew zeal for the Lord, lest similar discipline befall them.

The rest of Book IV provides a succinct overview and taste of the larger argument to come. In Books III–V Augustine reviewed the history of Rome and its gods, exposing the scurrilous, pernicious character of these false deities, as expressed in various cultural forms—notably, the stage plays—and complained about by even some of the pagan writers. Book V asserts the sovereignty of God against the spurious pagan claims of astrology and fate, and seems clearly intended to bolster the sagging faith of any of his Christian readers and to silence[16] any further spread of the pagan claims against the faith of Christ. In the opening of Book VI Augustine reported his satisfaction with that first installment. He felt confident that this first response to the pagan charges had been sufficient to quash any sympathy for those views and to staunch the flow of any lifeblood from the church to the pagan side:

> But as for such as read the said books without any obstinate intent, or
> with little, and ponder the things they read in an impartial discretion,

those shall approve that our labour in their satisfaction has rather
performed more than the question required otherwise: and that all
the malice, wherein they make Christianity the cause of all the af-
flictions falling upon this transitory world (the best learned of them
dissembling their knowledge against their own consciences), is not
only void of all reason and honesty, but fraught with light rashness
and pernicious impudence.[17]

Thus, the North African bishop appears to have been content that
his initial critique of the pagan charges had been sufficiently timely
and complete to have accomplished his hoped-for results.

A principled critique

Throughout the twenty-two books of *City of God*, Augustine
stayed focused on the charges and claims of Christianity's detractors,
examining them *in principle* to expose their fundamental unsoundness
vis-à-vis the majesty of the Christian faith. While from time to time
he attacked his opponents themselves—as when, in Book I, he chided
their cowardice and inconsistency in criticizing the very churches
that, as Rome was being sacked, provided a harbor of safety for them
against barbarian cruelty[18]—his overall method of criticism was to
set forth a charge or claim of the pagan position, examine it in the
light of history, culture, and other pagan writings, and demonstrate
the failure of the position as a viable contender for truth.

Let us consider one example, the claim that the pagan gods were
superior and that, in the sack of Rome, they were judging the religion
of Christ. This lie was easily exposed. Augustine simply pointed out
that the actual unfolding of events in Rome in those days indicated
quite the contrary. In fact, he explained, the barbarians actually spared
the Christians and their churches the great bulk of their havoc, which
they visited instead against the rest of the city; and, in spite of certain abuses, the barbarians protected those who claimed the name
of Christ—as well as any pagans who were shameless enough to lie
about their own convictions.[19] The record of events, Augustine argued,
disproved the claims of the pagans and cast doubt on the veracity of
their fundamental charge.

Further, the pagans had claimed that the Roman gods were noble,
decent, and good, and should not have been abandoned by the people
of Rome. In fact, Augustine pointed out, Rome had become "foully
bespotted with enormous impieties" prior to the coming of Christ,

while the ancient gods were still being venerated.[20] He pointed to
the obscene stage plays, which could be seen throughout the empire,
and other parts of the historical, cultural, and literary record, to
show that the gods, who were believed to have commissioned and
required these plays,[21] were actually to be despised for the filthiness
they promoted thereby. Not even the mothers of the gods—or of any
senator, honest man, or the stage players themselves—could watch
such demonstrations without embarrassment and disgust.[22] If you
reproach men when they do such wicked and filthy things, Augustine
asked, how can you accord them the status of gods who desire such
plays and "require it as part of their greatest honours to be cast in
the teeth with their own filthiness?"[23] The effects of these wicked
plays, and the honoring of those gods who commissioned them, was
to pollute the people of the empire with the wicked practices they
saw celebrated on the public stage.[24] Further, it was while those gods
were faithfully honored that Rome was rocked by such civil unrest
that violence and war tore at the very fabric of society:

> But let them blame their own gods for such mischiefs, that will not
> thank our Saviour Christ for any of His benefits. For whensoever they
> befell, their gods' altars steamed with Sabaean perfumes, and fresh
> flowers, and their priests were gallant, their temples shone, plays,
> sacrifices, and furies were all on foot amongst men; yea even when
> there was such an effusion of civil blood that the altars of the very
> gods were besprinkled with it.[25]

The ancient gods were vile and selfish; indeed, Augustine repeatedly
averred, they were no gods at all, but demons and malevolent spirits.
    Even those who taught the ways of the gods in public lectures
encouraged, if only by failure to condemn, "such horrible and abominable evils" that captured the minds of hearers and polluted their
bodies with wicked practices.[26] If you want true virtue, Augustine
pointed out, don't look to the defunct deities of Rome, or their apologists; go instead to listen to the words that are taught in any Christian church.[27] It was Christian preachers, unpacking the words of
the prophets and the apostles, who proclaimed a life of virtue and
excellence, and to whom the people, desperate for moral relief and
renewal, flocked in such great numbers.[28]
    Augustine's response to Christianity's pagan detractors proceeded
similarly along many fronts, as he examined the claims pagans made to

support their charges against the faith of Christ. The pagans claimed that only the Roman gods could give eternal life; that all the gods must be honored; that men were in the hands of fate unless they acknowledged the gods of Rome; and that everything about Roman philosophy, culture, and religion was superior to Christianity. One by one Augustine examined these various claims, showing them all to be without merit when compared with the teachings of Christ, and even, at times, using their own writers to bolster his case against them.[29]

A fair critique

Augustine was seeking to dismantle pagan charges against the Christian religion, and he would spare no argument in seeking to put his opponents' claims in the worst possible light. However, this did not mean that he would misrepresent their position, or that he would fail to acknowledge any truth that might be found in it. Augustine did not hesitate to point out that many of the pagan writers and thinkers of the past had "attained to truth"[30] in a variety of ways. He gave credit where it was due, especially when doing so enabled him to recruit pagan writers in support of his own views. He particularly found the works of Varro (116–27 BC) to be "acute and learned" and believed that, had the Romans taken him more seriously, he might have led them via philosophy to seek the knowledge of the true God.[31] Varro was generally acknowledged to be one of Rome's most learned men; Augustine appealed to his writings to support his contention that Roman religion was mere superstition, filled with "detestable absurdities."[32]

He also approved the views of the Platonists concerning the being of God against popular Roman religion and in support of the biblical notion of God as pure Spirit,[33] and he commended them as being closest to Christianity in their understanding of the greatest good as the knowledge of the one true God:[34]

> We choose the Platonists, being worthily held the most worthy of philosophers, because as they could conceive that the reasonable immortal soul of man could never be blessed but in participation in the light of God the world's Creator; so could they affirm that beatitude (the aim of all humanity) was unattainable without a firm adherence in pure love, unto the unchangeable One, that is, God.[35]

Augustine even found much that was good in Roman culture in general. He applauded the achievements of the Romans in arts and sciences, fashion, agriculture, navigation, animal husbandry, mathematics, and reasoning.[36] All these, he insisted, were evidences of the goodness of God, who gave men such abilities and allowed them to develop the good things of culture, even as they persisted in their ignorance of him, and then sent his Son for the redemption of their lost souls, in order that they might know true beauty and goodness in him.[37] Certainly, given the selfish and scurrilous character of the pagan gods, it was unreasonable to believe that they should in any way be credited with the achievements of Roman culture. As the best and most learned men of Rome had pointed out—and as the Christian religion had now made clear—that honor must be reserved for the One true God.

Augustine demonstrated that it was not necessary to exaggerate claims, distort facts, erect straw men, or otherwise seek by underhanded means to dismantle the arguments of one's opponents. By being fair concerning the truth that could be found in pagan views and achievements, he was able to enlist many of these in support of his rebuttal of the charges of Christianity's detractors.

A reasoned critique

The pagan detractors who blamed Christianity for the sack of Rome unpacked a raft of reasons why their charge should be accepted. They touted Rome's long years of peace and prosperity under the ancient gods, and the dignity and practicality of the Roman cult, insisting that the empire was a more civil and moral place before the rise of Christianity. Augustine examined each of these claims with a careful critique, appealing to the tenets of sound reason as he reviewed the historical, social, and cultural evidence against those claims. In the process, as Barker notes, Augustine was concerned "to provide a justification of the whole *philosophia Christi* in answer to the human philosophy of the ancient world."[38] Let us consider just two lines of Augustine's reasoned critique of the pagan claims and culture.

Augustine's first defense of the faith of Christ was to expose the hypocrisy of those railing against it. His argument proceeded along three lines. First, if he could undermine the credibility of Christianity's detractors, he would be more successful in dismantling all their claims. The pagans arriving in Hippo denounced Christianity as the reason for Rome's destruction; however, during the actual sack of Rome, many of them had found shelter from the barbarian wrath within the churches of the city, which had been designated as "safe zones" for those who fled there.[39] Perhaps Augustine saw a parable in this hypocrisy: the pagan Romans had themselves been kept alive by hiding in the shadow of the cross. Could they not see that this had been true of the empire itself?[40] His purpose in taking this tack was to call into question the judgment of the pagan detractors:

> And so escaped many then, that since have detracted from Christianity: they can impute their city's calamities wholly unto Christ, but that good which was bestowed on them only for Christ's honour (namely, the sparing of their lives) that they impute not unto our Christ, but unto their own fate; whereas if they had any judgment, they would rather attribute these calamities and miseries at the hands of their enemies all unto the providence of God, which is wont to reform the corruptions of men's manners by war and oppressions, and laudable to exercise the righteous in such afflictions; and having so tried them, either to transport them to a more excellent estate, or to keep them longer in the world for other ends and uses.[41]

In this quote Augustine summed up the whole of what he would unpack over the next thirteen years, as he assailed the bad judgment of the pagans, extolled the sovereign wisdom, power, and goodness of God, and called on his Christian readers to learn from this calamity how God would use them in the further progress of his kingdom.

Augustine took a second approach to exposing the hypocrisy of the pagans, this time using one of their own authorities against them. The pagans, it seemed, preferred the revels of the theaters (for Augustine, a symbol of the whole of degenerate pagan culture) to the sanctuaries of Christ—at least until their lives were at risk. But Scipio (184–129 BC) had refused to permit the stage plays during his consulship, because he feared they would encourage the people to practice immorality. Popular opinion prevailed, however, and the rest is history. But, Augustine was quick to point out:

> Hence comes it, that the mischiefs you yourselves commit, you are so loath should be imparted to yourselves, but the mischiefs that yourselves suffer, you are ever ready to cast upon the Christian profession, for you in your security do not seek the peace of the commonwealth, but freedom for your practice of luxury. You are depraved by prosperity, and you cannot be reformed by adversity.[42]

It is not difficult to see in this both a stinging rebuke to the hypocrisy of Christianity's detractors and a subtle admonition to any believers who might have been inclined to give credence to their claims. The real issue lying back of the pagan rant against Christianity was that the virtuous teaching of the gospel constrained their lascivious, self-indulgent ways—the ways of self-love, which, Augustine argued, was the defining feature of the City of Man. History had shown that those who would not listen to the voice of virtue—whether that of Christ or of the best men of Rome's past—would turn to self-indulgence, and that of the most scurrilous and violent kind. But when they themselves became the victim of the self-love of the barbarians, they would not have such "mischiefs" imputed as a failure of their worldview but, instead, looked to blame the faith of Christ. Is this a reasonable response to being subjected to adversity because of being depraved by prosperity? And for the Christian readers of this account, *caveat lector*.

There is yet a third line of attack against the hypocrisy of those who preferred the gods of the stage plays to the virtuous Lamb of God. If celebrating in public performances the degraded acts of the gods was such a good thing, Augustine wondered, why were those who performed the roles of those gods kept from the honor of citizenship in Rome? Why were stage players "counted as the worst rank of the members of thy city?"[43] Should not those who celebrated the acts of the gods be accorded the honors of the city that revered those gods? This was not the way of the Greeks; should not Rome have followed their illustrious forebears? Or did Roman practice lead to a more reasonable conclusion?

> Now in this disputation, this sole argument gives the upshot of the controversy. The Greeks propound: If such gods are to be worshipped, then such actors are also to be held as honourable. The Romans assume: But such actors are in no way to be held as honourable. The Christians conclude: Therefore such gods are in no way to be worshipped.[44]

A second aspect of Augustine's reasoned approach can be observed in Book V, in his powerful defense of the sovereignty of God as against the pagan claims of fortune or fate, and, in particular, astrology. Augustine strove to make the point that all the goodness men enjoy in this life comes from God, not from the false deities who were honored in the zodiac. Rome's long continuance was the result of God's forbearing goodness, and those who railed against him did so ungratefully, and to their shame. He insisted,

> But those that hold that the stars do manage our action, or our passions, good or ill, without God's appointment, are to be silenced and not to be heard, be they of the true religion, or be they bondslaves to idolatry of what sort soever; for what does this opinion do but flatly exclude all deity? Against the error, we profess not any disputation, but only against those that calumniate the Christian religion, in defence of their imaginary gods.[45]

Augustine's argument against this view took a number of tacks, including appeal to "scientific" considerations. He invited his readers to consider the example of twins—the many differences that appear in them, despite their having been born under the same constellation at the same time—as refutation of the claims of astrology.[46] He also pointed to the practice of those who believed in fate of laboring to select just the right days for such things as getting married and planting their crops. Why did they have to worry about getting this right, if fate had already determined at their births the course of things in their lives?[47] Did they expect later twists of fate to undo or improve former ones? If so, then what reason could they give for crediting fate with any power at all?

The remainder of Book V is devoted to asserting the sovereign goodness of God and to calling readers to credit him for all their good, and to rest in the knowledge of the goodness of the sovereign God in the midst of every crisis or time of uncertainty. He alone, and not the powerless fates or impersonal stars, is able to bring good to man in every situation. By many other such carefully reasoned responses did the Bishop of Hippo ably defend the faith of Christ against the pagan culture of his day.

A theological critique

The pagan detractors of Christianity preferred a worldview and culture that was ultimately theological in nature—as, indeed, are all worldviews and cultures, even the most putatively secular. In his response, Augustine could not simply ignore the pagan deities, even though he knew they were no gods at all. Instead, he drove straight at them in many ways and demonstrated their fecklessness and folly from the theology and history of Rome itself. The gods preferred by

Christianity's detractors, Augustine pointed out, were weak, immoral, irrational, inept, and downright silly. Only a fool would prefer such a theology to that of the beautiful Christ.

Augustine wondered aloud about how useful any gods could be who needed men to protect them: "would any wise man have commended the defence of Rome unto gods already proved unable to defend themselves?"[48] He further noted, citing works of Rome's venerable authorities, that the moral condition of the empire had begun to decay long before the coming of Christ, and asked, "But why did their gods look to this no better, nor help to save the state of the commonwealth, whose loss and ruin Cicero bewails with such pitiful phrase, long before Christ came in the flesh?"[49] Augustine summed up this part of his theological critique of Roman religion, advising Christianity's detractors,

> Let them choose which they like: if the gods be angry at men's keeping of their faith, let them seek faithless wretches to serve them. But if they that serve them and have their favours, be nevertheless afflicted and spoiled, then to what end are they adored? Wherefore let them hold their tongues that think they lost their city because they lost their gods; for though they had them all, they might nevertheless not only complain of misery, but feel it at full . . .[50]

Continuing his assault on the theology of Rome, Augustine exposed the utter silliness of the whole pagan pantheon. Why did the Romans need so many gods? he wondered. He playfully enumerated a few of the gods who, the Romans believed, attended to the details of their lives—everything from the skies and seas to the care and feeding of children, the alleviating of fears, learning to count, and even the hairs on our chins. Was not Jupiter sufficient for all their needs? If they had to have some deity or other to venerate for every detail of life, then how much power could the supreme father of the gods actually have? Or are all the lesser gods merely "parts and virtues of him"? In which case, why not simplify matters and follow the lead of the Christians in worshipping the one true God?[51] And, in a lengthy diatribe in Book III, Augustine exposed the utter uselessness of the gods, who had been altogether unable to prevent "the miserable state of Rome" leading up to the Second Punic War. The withering, "Where were they?" repeated over and over in this chapter, must have been a devastating embarrassment to any so foolish as to recommend the gods of Rome over the all-sovereign, all-good God of the Christians.[52] Roman theology, which the pagan detractors of Christianity were so foolish to propose as more desirable than the gospel of Christ, was thus exposed as altogether bankrupt.

An evangelical critique

In the sixth place, the Bishop of Hippo took every opportunity to point his readers to the glories of the Christian faith and of the gospel of Jesus Christ. His apologetic is woven throughout with citations from scripture and brief elaborations of the Good News concerning Jesus and the kingdom of God. As Ernest Barker observes, for Augustine, "criticism was not enough: St. Augustine desired to be constructive as well as destructive; he desired not only to put to flight pagan murmurings about the sack of Rome, but also to draw over to the Christian side the thoughtful pagan . . . who was pondering the truth of Christian evidences."[53] Augustine proclaimed Jesus as the only hope for miserable men to realize communion with the one true God.

In Book IX Augustine mused on the misery of man and his perpetual longing to be connected with transcendent reality, reviewing the works of philosophers and the history of Roman experience to demonstrate that nothing in Rome's theology or philosophy had been able to satisfy this universal longing. Men, according to Roman views, were too much flesh, and the gods were too much spirit for there to be any true converse between them. What was to be done? For,

> if that be true (which is far more probable) that all men of necessity must be miserable whilst they are mortal, then must a mean be found which is God as well as man, who by the mediation of this blessed mortality may help us out of this mortal misery unto that immortal happiness: and this man must be born mortal, but not continue so.[54]

This, he continued, is what Jesus Christ has done, whom the pagan detractors vilify in their accusations against the Christian faith. Only Jesus can fulfill our need for a mediator, for only he partakes of both body and spirit, of the most pure kind ("his blessed mortality"), and is thus acceptable both to God and man for the redemption of miserable mortals. "This, as the scripture proclaims, is the Mediator between God and man, the man Christ Jesus . . ."[55]

But how could this be so? How does Jesus accomplish this mediation that all men earnestly seek? At the beginning of Book X,

Augustine pointed out, developing the arguments of the Platonists concerning what is reasonable in offering service to God, a sacrifice was obviously necessary. God is pleased with sacrifice, as even pagan philosophy and religion acknowledge, but it must be just the right one if we are truly to commune with him. Animal sacrifices will not suffice, as everyone seemed to know, and as the scriptures declare. A perfect sacrifice was needed, and this is precisely what Jesus has provided.[56] Thus, Jesus satisfied the requirements of God and man, and became "the universal way" for people of every nation to escape the misery of fallen humanity and be reconciled with God.[57] So, rather than vilify this One whom God sent for our redemption, miserable, fallen men must flee to him as a safe harbor against all manner of evil, both now and in the day of judgment (a theme fully developed in Book XX).

Faith is the way to benefit from the mediation Jesus has accomplished. But it must be true faith, not insincere. That is, it must be faith proven in life, and not just a faith expressed for some momentary relief from distress—like fleeing to the churches in the face of the barbarian hordes. Augustine was consistently clear on this demand of the gospel:

> Now whoever has Christ in his heart, even though he desire temporal things (and sometimes things lawful), still possesses Christ for the foundation thereof. But if he prefer these things before Christ, though he seem to hold his faith, yet Christ is no foundation in him, in that he prefers those vanities to Him. And if he both contemn good instruction, and prosecute bad actions, how much the sooner shall he be convicted of setting Christ at naught, and esteeming Him of no value in vainer respects, by neglecting His command and allowance, and in contempt of both, following his own lustful extravagance.[58]

Wherever in the course of his rebuttal of the pagan charges the context and argument allowed the Bishop of Hippo to declare some aspect of the good news of Jesus, he was quick to do so, showing at every point how Jesus was the fulfillment of the hopes and aspirations of miserable men, hopes and aspirations that Roman philosophy and theology acknowledged, but could not satisfy. *City of God* does not build its way toward the proclamation of the gospel at the end of all argumentation; rather, it returns again and again to the good news of Jesus as the answer to the human crisis at every turn.

A visionary critique

Finally, Augustine's critique of Roman worldview and theology is set in the context of a glorious vision of the city to come, the eternal hope of the Christian faith. As Barker noted concerning *City of God*,

> This is what makes the work one of the great turning-points in the history of human destiny: it stands on the confines of two worlds, the classical and the Christian, and it points the way into the Christian. For there is never a doubt, in all the argument, from the first words of the first chapter of the first book, of the victory of that "most glorious city of God" proclaimed, as with the voice of a trumpet, in the very beginning and prelude.[59]

Once again, as Barker notes, this theme of the grandeur and coming glory of the city of God permeates the whole of Augustine's critique. All hope men may have of knowing anything of true virtue and peace in this life depends on their seeing clearly into the unseen things of the city that is to come. But he especially develops his vision of the coming city in Book XIX, showing how the city of God and all it promises and portends fulfill the hope of Rome's best thinkers for realizing the greatest good, and motivate the citizens of that city to virtuous and peaceable living here and now.

After showing that Rome's best thinkers—Varro, especially—could only conceive of the greatest good in temporal and material terms, Augustine pointed out that no one seeking that end in this life has been able to attain it.[60] The greatest good is not to be found in the experience of the body, but in the liberating of the spirit, so that men may not be made miserable by any temporal pains but, freed from all manner of lust, may enter into the true happiness of the city of God. The greatest good that men can know, therefore, can never be realized in time and space; rather, we must seek the city that is to come, where we will know the presence and glory of God and be set free from all temporal and material restraints. For now, we must set our hearts and minds on the attaining of that objective, for, as we meditate on this greatest good, and focus on him who provides it, we will be more inclined to serve him in this life, and thus to express the love of God and neighbor here and now, which are the defining features of the city of God.[61]

As men long and hope for the city to come they find the strength and wisdom to live sociably and justly here and now.[62] They pursue virtue in this life, since this is the end for which they have been made, and their virtue enables them to sow peace amid the troubles and turmoil of a world ravaged by the devil.[63] Obedience to the law of God on the part of the members of God's city produces peace, as love for God and neighbor increases on the earth. Through obedience they break the hold of sin, which drags men down into servitude and injustice, and bring to partial reality on earth that which can be fully realized only in the age to come.[64] Thus, the citizens of the heavenly city live in this life like everyone else, with the same needs, participating, in many ways, in the same culture; yet they are distinguished by true and unshakeable hope, which produces virtue, justice, and happiness.[65] Christ alone is able to provide such hope. Through him alone we have entrance to and become members of the city to come, and pursue our earthly pilgrimage in virtue and peace until he comes to receive us unto himself.[66] In this life we may know partial peace, but full and undying hope. In that hope of unending bliss and joy the members of God's city pursue their pilgrimage amid the miseries of a sinful world, and are thus a source of peace and virtue for all:

> Man's righteousness therefore is this: to have God his Lord, and himself His subject; his soul master over his body; and his reason over sin, either by subduing it or resisting it; and to entreat God both for His grace and merit, and His pardon for sin, and lastly to be grateful for all His bestowed graces. But in that final peace, unto which all man's peace and righteousness on earth has reference, immortality and incorruption do so refine nature from viciousness, that there we shall have no need of reason to rule over sin, for there shall be no sin at all there, but God shall rule man, and the soul the body; and obedience there shall be as pleasant and easy, as the state of them that live shall be glorious and happy.[67]

Book XXII, the final installment in this thirteen-year project, develops more fully the vision of the city that is to come and makes a final, powerful appeal to all readers to turn to Jesus and enter into the hope that cannot fade. A day of judgment and resurrection is coming; let men prepare for it now. The witness of the martyrs testifies to the truth of Christ. The good gifts of God to all men summon them to seek him with thankful hearts. All the philosophers hoped for an eternal state of happiness that can be found only in Christ, and that will surely be realized by the faithful at the end of the age, in the new heavens and the new earth, before the presence of the beautiful and glorious God and Jesus Christ, whom we shall see face to face:

> There we shall rest and see, we shall see and love, we shall love and we shall praise. Behold what shall be in the end without end! For what other thing is our end, but to come to that kingdom of which there is no end?[68]

All seven of these aspects of Augustine's response to Christianity's detractors—his critique of their claims and culture—are woven together in a continuous cord throughout the pages of *City of God*. His insights provide a valuable template for believers today as we seek to discover aspects of a renewed consensus on culture matters and take up the task of keeping watch over the culture around us.

A Contemporary Exemplar: *First Things*

We cannot escape involvement with culture; and, since not all the culture that presses upon us day by day is useful to us in our calling to seek first the kingdom of God and his righteousness, we must learn to look beyond the mere appearances of contemporary culture—that which attracts, entertains, delights, informs, and so forth—to the deeper worldview issues of culture, and we must learn to judge with righteous judgment the culture in which we participate in our day. We must develop and sustain an ongoing dialogue with and critique of the culture in which we live.

But we may not expect to do this, as Jonathan Edwards might have said, "by the bye." The task of keeping watch on the culture around us requires active vigilance on our parts, a conscious effort to observe, assess, expose, communicate, and countermand the aspects of contemporary culture that oppose the progress of the kingdom of God, as well as to appreciate and affirm, and show the way in how to employ, those elements of contemporary culture that we may use with benefit in our kingdom endeavors. Unless we are each willing to take up a position on the walls of God's city, there to exercise vigilance on behalf of our friends and to keep watch against whatever threats may arise, we shall find that we are more often admitting the enemies of the kingdom into our very midst, rather than exposing and resisting them as Augustine did so ably in his generation.[69] This task is made even more urgent in our day by the presence of a rapidly expanding, kudzu-like pop culture, which threatens to overwhelm and transform all other culture, including that of the Christian community, into its own image. Surely the first plank in the platform of a consensus among Christians toward culture matters is that we agree to join together in keeping watch over the culture of our day, and that we nurture and sustain an energetic, lively, and effective critique of contemporary culture from the perspective of our biblical worldview. Such a commitment will require time, effort, and guidance from those who are already practicing this important discipline.

Happily, in this latter area there are many helpful places to which we may turn. A wide variety of resources exists that can help us in developing a Christian critique of contemporary culture. Besides the increasing numbers of conferences, seminars, and workshops addressing aspects of a Christian response to contemporary culture, many helpful publications and periodicals are readily available. Among the latter, Ken Myers's *Mars Hill Audio Journal* is a valuable resource, offering reviews, interviews, and criticism of contemporary cultural trends from the perspective of a biblical worldview. *Christianity Today's Books & Culture* magazine is another such resource. Each issue contains timely reviews and essays that can help to develop our ability to understand the times and know what we as God's people should do (1 Chron. 12:32). *BreakPoint Worldview,* a publication of the BreakPoint division of Prison Fellowship Ministries, offers monthly editorials, essays, commentaries, and reviews on a wide range of culture matters. *World* magazine, *Touchstone, Re:Generation Quarterly,*[70] *The Christian Century,* and *Christianity Today* can also be helpful in developing a Christian critique of contemporary culture.

Chief among these resources as representing what we might consider an "Augustinian" critique of contemporary culture is the journal *First Things,* a publication of the Institute for Religion and Public Policy in New York, edited by Fr. Richard John Neuhaus. *First Things* is an ecumenical journal of opinion, offering brief editorials, reasoned articles, book reviews, lively interchanges with correspondents, and the running social and cultural commentary of Fr. Neuhaus with each monthly issue (except June/July and August/September). *First Things* is a serious, but not a scholarly, journal; footnotes are forbidden. Most of the articles and reviews can be read in a single sitting, although many of them deserve more prolonged rereading and consideration.

First Things has sustained a consistent and trenchant critique of contemporary culture and society from its beginning. Firmly rooted in the great tradition of historic Christian faith, and employing contributors from across the spectrum of Christian orthodoxy, *First Things* speaks with a biblically grounded and theologically informed voice about every aspect of life and culture. Its writers include Roman Catholics, Orthodox, evangelicals, Pentecostals, and representatives from other faith traditions from time to time, all of whom share the common conviction of believing together what the church has taught in every age and at every place.

It would be difficult to name any aspect of culture that *First Things* has not addressed at some point in its brief history. From just one recent year alone contributors have held forth on matters of Christian unity, church/state relations, the state of American culture, developments in contemporary psychological thinking and practice, the Internet, science and faith, the law of God, the great tsunami of 2004 and the storms of 2005, historical persons and events of significance for contemporary Christians, matters of theology and apologetics, developments in schools and courts and legislatures across the land, piety and spiritual disciplines, war and peace, international developments, presidential politics, comparative religion, the death penalty, biotechnological developments, the Supreme Court, and much, much more. As with Augustine, the critique of contemporary culture *First Things'* writers bring to their task is timely, just what Christians need to be thinking about in order to avoid being overwhelmed by the flood of naturalistic and postmodern thinking welling up around them. Its writers present principled, fair, and reasoned discussions, and readers are always invited to enter the conversation, either by way of letters to the editor or in discussion groups of their own. Readers of *First Things* have become so numerous, and are spread so broadly across the spectrum of contemporary Christianity, that they have begun to organize into local discussion groups—*ROFTERS* ("Readers of *First Things*"; the editors are happy to help in organizing such groups). Like Augustine, *First Things* presents an unapologetically theological and evangelical critique of culture matters, and casts a vision for the difference a consistent Christian approach to such matters might make. Careful readers can come away from any essay, article, or review with clear and cogent insights to reform their own approach to culture matters, as well as compelling "talking points" for advancing a biblical view of culture matters in conversation with their contemporaries.

This lively and intelligent journal makes for stimulating and insightful reading each month, beginning (as I always do) with Fr. Neuhaus's running commentary on culture matters, "The Public Square." *First Things* makes no bones about it: culture matters, and the state of things in culture matters today is such that Christians need to be alert, informed, and disciplined to interact critically with culture, so that we may together begin to forge new paths of obedience amid the weeds and wilds of unbelieving cultural activity in our day. Those eager to develop an approach to culture matters that is truthful, gracious, alluring, persuasive, evangelical, and enduring—in a word, Augustinian—could do no better than to take up a subscription to *First Things* and join the growing ranks of those whose cultural involvement is being shaped and formed by the best writers in the contemporary church.[71]

A Christian approach to culture begins with a thoughtful, ongoing critique of the issues and events of our day, in conversation with like-minded believers who seek above all else to preserve the light of truth and grace in a day of decadence and doubt. The barbarians are threatening to overwhelm the once-glorious culture bequeathed to us in the West by our Christian forebears and those who fell under their wise and gracious sway. We who would recover that heritage and advance it for subsequent generations must join together to assess the damage, sort out the riches from the rot, and begin to think about ways of creating new culture together. Culture matters, and the careful critique of culture matters, according to an Augustinian paradigm, is, it seems to me, the place to begin in forging greater unity, consensus, and fruitfulness in this critical, inescapable area of life.

Questions for Study or Discussion

1. Our involvement with culture necessarily requires the use of certain criteria for judging culture—values, tastes, impressions, goals, and so forth. In your own use of culture (fashion, entertainment, personal development, vocation, etc.), what criteria do you presently employ to judge the culture in which you are involved?

2. Look back over the seven criteria Augustine used in evaluating the claims of those who touted Roman culture over that of the church. Explain each of these in your own words:

- timely:

- principled:

- fair:

- reasoned:

- theological:

- evangelical:

- visionary:

3. Review the definitions you provided above. For each of them, using a scale of 1 to 10 (where 1 = "not at all" and 10 = "at all times"), assign a number indicating the extent to which you presently employ these aspects of a critique of culture in your own approach to judging culture. Why did you choose the numbers you did?

4. What resources do you presently employ to help you judge the culture in which you are involved? To what extent, and in what ways, do the resources of your faith—the Bible, writings of other Christians, conversations with Christian friends—help to form your approach to culture matters?

5. What do you hope to gain from this study of culture matters? What goals would you like to set for yourself as you read this book? What will tell you, when you have reached the end of this study, that you have benefited from it?

Forging New Culture

Celtic Christian Art and the Rebirth of Culture in an Age of Darkness

The artist cannot wait, in fact nobody can, till the world is renewed, the crisis solved, and new cultural principles worked out. We have to participate in the life of our times. In fact the artist might even stand in the most difficult place, as the spirit of anti-Christianity, of dehumanization, of despair is strongest in the avant-garde tradition of the arts. But maybe there is still something left of the strong old traditions that can be used as a starting point.

H. R. Rookmaaker

Every good gift and every perfect gift is from above, coming down from the Father of lights with whom there is no variation or shadow due to change.

James 1:17

AUGUSTINE'S THOROUGH CRITIQUE of the pagan culture of his day came at the beginning of a dark period in European history. Even as the great saint lay dying, the barbarians were at the door, and they would sweep over the entire vast expanse of Rome's European empire, with nothing cultural to contribute but plunder, stasis, and, ultimately, decline. A nomadic and militaristic people, the Germanic tribes that supplanted traditional Roman rule cared only for order and power. They had little interest in intellectual elegance or cultural achievement: the greatest Christian philosopher of the fifth century, Boethius, was brutally martyred by the barbarian emperor he sought to serve. The darkness that settled on the western part of Rome's crumbling empire during the fourth and fifth centuries was nearly total. Only here and there did cultural lights flicker as reminders of the glory that once was.

Yet even as the darkness was deepening on the European mainland, a fresh phoenix of culture was rising from the ashes of another ancient, dying way of life, among the wild Celtic peoples of Ireland and Scotland, who, heirs of a rich, albeit illiterate, cultural heritage, had come into possession of the light of truth through the impetus provided by the missionary Patrick and others from the mid-fifth century on. For the Celtic Christians of the sixth through the ninth centuries, their pagan heritage, for all its crudity and simplicity, became the platform for constructing a new culture that would play a significant role in bringing revival and renewal to many parts of the Western church. Consisting of a vast literary and artistic achievement, sound community structure, and a highly disciplined spirituality, the legacy of Celtic Christianity comes down to us today, among other things, in the heritage of Celtic Christian art. The astonishing legacy of the Celtic Christians was an unlikely achievement. It arose from the ashes of antiquity amid the darkness of barbarianism to shine the brilliant light of Christian culture throughout a weary continent. In the work of these anonymous artists we see an example of how visionary believers can forge new culture out of the rubble and bring beauty, goodness, and truth to life in a time of uncertainty and despair.

We have all seen and loved various expressions of ancient Celtic Christian art. The "circle crosses" in many Anglican and Presbyterian churches, decorative interlocking keys and knots, flowing designs in jewelry and clothing, and delicate and often surreal flora and fauna: these are just a few of the cultural forms surviving from one of the most prolific and important periods in the heritage of Christian culture. While not the earliest expression of the use of art for Christian purposes, the arts that flourished among the Celtic peoples of Europe from the sixth to the ninth centuries are a good place for us to turn as we pursue our discussion of culture matters toward the discovery of principles for an authentic contemporary Christian cultural consensus. For not only must we necessarily engage culture, ready to judge it with righteous judgment, but we must *create* culture as well, and not just in the arts. The language we speak, the manners we use, our ways of relating in families, among friends, and on the job, as well as our tastes in cultural forms and diversions—all these and more we both engage and recreate, for our own generation and for those who will succeed us. We must be concerned, therefore, not just for exercising an effective cultural watch, but for the culture we create as well, and the ways we go about creating it. Our Celtic Christian forebears have left us an example for creating culture that contains many sound principles to guide us through the maze of culture matters.

The current renaissance of interest in Celtic Christianity is an encouraging sign, suggesting as it does a renewed curiosity concerning the Christian past and the lessons it might hold for us today.[1] What Robert Wilken has written about Christian intellectuals is surely true of all Christians, that we are "inescapably bound to those persons and ideas and events that have created the Christian memory."[2] The prevalence of Celtic themes in contemporary film, pop culture, and literature has helped to promote widespread awareness of this important period.

The Celtic Revival

The period of the Celtic revival—roughly the middle of the fifth to the end of the eighth centuries, a little over three hundred years—is especially rich in literature, artifacts, stories, and lessons to enrich our understanding and appreciation of the Christian past and to guide us in the work of formulating a Christian consensus on culture matters. Thomas Cahill is not far from the mark in his claim that Irish missionary-monks saved Western civilization from barbaric inundation. Not only in their evangelistic zeal, but in their profound and earnest piety, love of books and learning, strong sense of community, and commitment to a distinctively Christian expression of their Celtic cultural heritage, generations of "wanderers for Christ," together with the people who populated the communities they founded, helped to preserve the Christian heritage of the early church and to lay again the foundations of civil society after the catastrophe of barbarism.

Celtic Christian art is undoubtedly what most people think of as the outstanding achievement of this period. Indeed, it is a significant achievement. Lavish and exquisitely illustrated biblical manuscripts, immense stone crosses, elegant liturgical vessels, and delicate everyday artifacts reveal a common sense of vision and purpose and a common devotion to excellence and innovation, within a common artistic tradition, that is unsurpassed in the history of Christian artistic endeavor. Building on the foundations of their Celtic heritage, and borrowing freely from existing Christian and non-Christian cultures, Celtic artists managed to forge a completely new culture during the most unlikely of cultural seasons. We can learn from them to resist the temptation to despair over the state of contemporary culture or to wait until things improve before we take up the task of renewing culture and working for a Christian consensus on culture matters. The Celtic Christian artists of the past can encourage us to take up this challenge with vigor and vision.

After first defining what we understand by the term "Celtic Christian art," we will then examine the lasting achievement of those ancient Celtic artists, before offering some observations concerning how they might help us in taking up the task of achieving Christian consensus over culture matters. We'll also chat with Phil Keaggy, a contemporary Christian artist whose *oeuvre* in many ways embodies the pioneering spirit of our Celtic predecessors.

Celtic Christian Art

"Celtic Christian art" describes a category of ancient abstract religious art, concentrated chiefly in early medieval Ireland and Britain, that incorporates elements of pure form, floral and faunal representationalism, and biblical and hagiographical iconography, and is expressed within an impressive range of media, principally everyday domestic and personal objects, various kinds of liturgical vessels, magnificent illustrated manuscripts, and imposing carved crosses.[3]

Ancient abstract art

Celtic Christian art is a form of abstract art. It makes wide use of geometric forms and patterns, spirals singular and in combination, especially triskeles, interlocking patterns of steps and keys, stylized twisted crosses, and varieties of lacework. Its plant and animal forms are highly exaggerated and frequently employed in pairs or as parts of larger patterns in which their forms and bodies are contorted into impossible shapes that are nonetheless logical and beautiful given the larger context in which they appear. Even the human figures in Celtic Christian art—the saints and biblical characters who feature so prominently, especially on carved crosses—are deliberately presented in the abstract, but not merely because these artists were incapable of doing better.[4] Cut off from developments in the rest of Christian art,[5] Christian artists in Ireland and Britain drew from their existing cultural heritage, their contacts with neighboring cultures, and their sense of Christian cultural responsibility to create new and enduring forms that continue to enthrall, "one of the great artistic traditions of the world and one which, furthermore, retained its integrity for more than fifteen hundred years."[6]

J. Romilly Allen has nicely summarized the leading characteristics of Celtic Christian art as follows:[7]

1. The prominence given to the margin or frame within which the whole design is enclosed.
2. The arrangement of the design within the margin in panels, each containing a complete piece of ornament.
3. The use of setting-out lines for the ornament, placed diagonally with regard to the margin.
4. The use of interlaced-work, step-patterns, key-patterns, spirals, and zoomorphs in combination.
5. The geometrical perfection of all the ornaments.
6. The superiority of the decorative designs to the figure drawing.

To these I would add (7) an assiduous concern for economy of space and an abhorrence of artistic vacuum, a crowding, but not cluttering, of the artistic surface.[8] Allen's sixth point must also be regarded in the light of the earlier comments about abstraction, given that he was writing prior to the development of abstract arts in this century. On the whole, however, Allen's summary fairly captures the artistic elements common to Celtic Christian art in all its forms throughout this period.

Art forms

There are numerous excellent examples of Celtic Christian art, and the range of genre in which they occur is impressive. There are, first of all, domestic and personal everyday objects. Celtic Christians crafted their art for the personal use and adornment of members of the Christian community. They recognized, in the elegant brooches, buckles, mirrors, and other everyday items they created, the importance of culture in everyday life. Next are the liturgical vessels: plates, chalices, croziers, bells, and reliquaries. Most impressive, however, are the illustrated manuscripts—the Lindisfarne Gospels and the Books of Kells chief among these—and the immense stone crosses, such as at Moone and Monasterboice in Ireland. These last, in particular, reveal not only the artistic genius of these Celtic Christians, but their theological convictions as well. Green writes of these last two forms especially,

> Such art transcended the need for words, the Christian doctrine was conveyed, above all, by visual expression. Christian Celtic art has been likened to the great sacred choral works of Bach and others, where the words sung are less important than the glory of the music itself. The skill of the early Christian artists, together with their beliefs and innermost feelings, were poured into a visual expression of awe, love and reverence which was as eloquent as any human or animal sacrifice offered to the gods in the pagan Celtic period.[9]

While not all forms of Celtic Christian art, particularly those produced for domestic or personal use, are specifically religious or Christian, nonetheless, their use of common elements, forms, and themes, in the context of early medieval Christian Ireland and Britain, marks them as part of a common vision, heritage, and tradition.

The Celtic Christian Achievement

There is much to learn, to take delight in, from the Celtic Christian artists, whose many enduring works helped to sustain and advance the work of God's kingdom during the period of the medieval church. Five aspects in particular of the Celtic Christian achievement in the arts are noteworthy.

Forging a new tradition

First, these artists, cut off from formal developments in Christian art elsewhere, and working in a context of degenerating culture and literacy, managed to forge a new and enduring artistic tradition out of their common cultural heritage, contact with other contemporary cultures, and deep religious conviction. The Celtic artists who left us such rich treasures were the heirs of an artistic tradition that had its roots in the preliterate, pre-Christian Celtic cultures of Europe and the Western Isles. These Celtic craftsmen of earlier generations were excellent workers in brass, gold, and glass, and left treasure troves of artistic finery in the forms of everyday vessels, swords and scabbards and shield bosses, and religious artifacts in burial mounds and other sites in Europe, Britain, and Ireland. On many of these pieces can be found forms, motifs, and techniques that would ultimately find their way into the art of the Celtic Christians, who recognized the good gifts of God to their Celtic forebears and freely appropriated them for their own art.

On the foundation of that long-standing tradition, Celtic Christian artists incorporated elements from other cultures with which their missionary-monks made contact. These included German, Scandinavian, and even Mediterranean cultures.[10] Taking from the arts of these cultures whatever suited their tastes and purposes and could be made to harmonize with their essentially Celtic heritage, Celtic Christian artists brought into being an altogether new artistic tradition. Michael Ryan has written concerning these various influences on Celtic Christian artists,

> All of these enabled the monastic houses to foster a new hybrid art which, with variations, was shared by manuscript illuminators, metalworkers and later, monumental sculptors, in northern Britain and Ireland. In this art, Ultimate La Tene scrollwork remained a vital decorative element, but during the seventh century, filigree, complex casting imitating deep engraving, die-stamping of decorative foils, gilding and granulation were also borrowed by Celtic craftsmen from the Germanic world and, with these, they produced dazzling and highly colourful work.[11]

In so doing the Celtic Christians were merely following the practices of their ancestors, who borrowed freely from the cultures they encountered to create an art suitable to their tastes and purposes.[12] But also, like the Israelites despoiling the Egyptians or Solomon drawing from the artistic materials, skills, and traditions of Tyrian culture, the Celtic Christian artists drew from the excellence they had inherited as well as that which they encountered in the cultures of their day to bring into being a uniquely Christian expression of their Celtic cultural heritage. As Allen observed,

> I cannot see that it in the least detracts from the praise due to the originators of the style if it can be shown that the ideas underlying many of the patterns were suggested by a pre-existing native style or adapted from a foreign one. Interlaced-work, key-patterns, spirals, and zoomorphs are to be found separately in the decorative art of many races and many periods, but nowhere and at no time have these different elements been used in combination with such consummate skill, as in the early Christian period in Great Britain and Ireland.[13]

Taking contemporary culture captive for Christ

Closely related to this first aspect of the Celtic Christian achievement is the second. The Celtic Christians managed to take over for decidedly Christian purposes the artistic achievements of their Celtic tradition and their foreign contemporaries. The common triskele, and other forms used in triples, would be used as a constant reminder of the glory of the triune God. Images of the sun, frequent in pagan pre-Christian cultures, were positioned to represent Christ, the Sun of Righteousness. Proven techniques were turned to Christian purposes in the creation of art. Free-standing stone megaliths, pagan symbols of the center of the world and the connecting-point to the realm of the spiritual, were transformed into massive carved crosses declaring unmistakably Christian messages. Methods used to create expensive jewelry for pagan elites were adopted to illustrate the gospel books of monks and their students. Delicate Celtic ornamentation was engraved on chalices and communion plates to heighten communicants' sense of the presence, beauty, and glory of God.

There is no sense in which these Celtic Christian artists can be accused of making a way for paganism in their art. What Derek Bryce has written of the carved cross is equally true of Celtic art in general: "there is no question of paganism infiltrating Christianity, but simply of Christianity adopting a form of symbolism which is universal," and, we add, using it for its particular purposes.[14]

In Celtic Christian art, therefore, we have a remarkable example of Christians endeavoring to apply the Apostle Paul's instruction to take every thought captive and make it obedient to Christ, even those that are manifestly opposed to the knowledge of the one, true God (2 Cor. 10:3–5).

Creating a new narrative

The third aspect of the achievement of the Celtic Christian artists, founded on the first and the second, is that they transformed an essentially non-narrative art into one that powerfully declares a biblical and Christian worldview.[15] This is especially true of the massive carved crosses that began to appear toward the middle of this period. Jakob Streit has written, "It was the task of the monks to illustrate and emphasize their connection with the Christian mystery by means of such illustrated crosses, for the novices and for the people."[16] The same, however, could be said of illustrated manuscripts and even common objects, for Christian symbols and symbols from existing sources that were made to serve the Christian purposes of the artists appear throughout Celtic Christian art.[17]

The message of Celtic Christian art is essentially one of the biblical teaching concerning the victory of Christ and his rule over all the elements of creation.[18] As Hilary Richardson says, Celtic Christian art "was not so much religious art as liturgical, expressing the Church's experience of God. It was an art constructed to aid contemplation and prayer."[19] Celtic Christians are remembered for their deep spirituality, and they expressed the fundamentals of their piety in the art with which they adorned their settlements and places of worship. They have left us an unmistakable message concerning the convictions that motivated their evangelistic, communal, and cultural endeavors.

Inventing new art forms

In the fourth place it is the achievement of Celtic Christian artists to have invented two entirely new art forms, the illustrated manuscript and the carved cross. While illustration in manuscripts, as well as manufactured crosses, can be found in earlier art, there is nothing to compare with the freestanding Irish cross or the illustrated gospel books of the Celtic Christians.

The carved crosses seem to have been taken over from pagan megaliths, the victory of Christ being substituted for pagan myths about the spiritual world and how to connect with it.[20] These crosses served as teaching tools and focal points of devotion for Celtic Christians, much as their megalith predecessors had served their pagan ancestors. But in the hands of Celtic Christian sculptors the message became that the resurrected Christ is the meeting-place between heaven and earth, the only One worthy of worship and devotion. As Philip Sheldrake has observed, "If we ask what the purpose of the crosses was, the clearest answer is that they existed simply to testify to the Christian faith."[21] Thus, the creators of carved crosses seem to have had a kind of sacramental purpose in mind for their art.

Celtic illuminated manuscripts, of which the Lindisfarne Gospels and the Book of Kells are the quintessential examples, are without peer in the history of this genre. Not only are the carpet pages, the portraits of the evangelists, and the elaborate initials exquisite in design, detail, and color, but the text itself is beautiful. The script of these illustrated manuscripts—called the insular majuscule—became the standard for manuscripts throughout all of Britain and the areas of Europe evangelized by Irish missionary-monks.[22] Thus, the influence of Celtic Christian artists was felt each time a monk transcribed a text, read his devotions, or taught the laypeople or novices under his care.

Demonstrating a commitment to excellence

Finally, it was the achievement of the Celtic Christian artists to have demonstrated a commitment to excellence in artistic endeavor that serves as a standard for Christian artists of all ages. These largely unknown artists were devoted to honoring God with their labors.[23] There could be no place for shoddiness or for merely making-do in their work. Anyone who considers the fine detail and demanding craftsmanship of the Tara Brooch, Eadfrith's carefully conceived and brilliantly executed plan for the Lindisfarne Gospels, or the placement and combination of figures and forms on the Moone cross cannot fail to appreciate both the thoughtfulness and the brilliance of technique that went into the execution of these pieces. These were not the result of mass fabrication, pieces of art rushed into production in order to capitalize on a present demand. The artifacts of the Celtic Christian artists show a concern that God be glorified in even the smallest detail of the work, no matter how long that might take or how tedious and demanding the labor might be.

As Allen has observed, "the beauty and individuality of the ornamental designs found in early Christian art in Great Britain are due chiefly to the great taste with which the different elements are combined and the exquisite finish lavished upon them."[24] This combination of taste, design, and execution continues to serve as a standard for artists today.

Lessons for Christian Artists Today

Having thus briefly defined Celtic Christian art and summarized the achievement of the artists of this period, it remains for us to suggest some ways in which contemporary Christian artists, and the Christian community as a whole, might benefit from a more careful study of this subject for the purpose of renewing culture and working toward a Christian consensus on culture matters. What lessons do the persons, ideas, and artistic legacy of this period offer to contemporary Christians? Briefly, I would like to suggest seven.

Make certain of your message

First, the example of the Celtic Christian artists suggests that Christians involved in culture matters today must make certain of their message. One of the enduring elements of Celtic Christian art, and one that made it such a powerful educational and liturgical tool in its own day—without, I hasten to add, compromising beauty, integrity, or originality—is its prophetic character. Celtic Christian art had a message to declare, and it proclaimed that message clearly and powerfully to generations who were familiar with the images, themes, and forms these artists employed.

Today the trend in culture matters is toward a relativism that obscures any sense of abiding truth. Emphasis is on the personal meaning that the artist encodes into his or her work, as well as the spectator's subjective encounter with that work. The idea of any "metanarrative" to art, that art has a story to tell, is denied.[25] This theme easily translates into all areas of culture, reducing the work of culture to little more than an exercise in taste, whether our involvement is in the arts or in such everyday endeavors as language, manners, or ethics. We need merely reflect on the deterioration of language and conversation, the decline of civility, and the fragile state of families in our own culture to see the effects on cultural activity of the loss of a commanding narrative. Christians seeking a perspective on culture matters may experience a strong pull toward nonobjectivity or mere individualism, or pure innovation. As a result, they may forgo any spiritual emphasis, message, or encounter as somehow inappropriate or impossible, at least in polite company or the public square. Similarly, Christians may be tempted to seek little more than some satisfying subjective experience through their involvement in culture, some burst of pleasure, without any reference to the deeper, more universal meaning that can be conveyed through a work of art, a song, a film, or a poem.

This is not to suggest that our cultural activities should not contain a strongly personal element. Taste in culture matters will always leave room for individual expression and preference. However, mere taste, or undisciplined taste, taste that follows every merely personal whim, apart from any larger narrative, can be destructive of true culture, whether in the arts, language, making a family, or pursuing a career. Such an approach to culture matters compromises the larger Christian calling to let our light so shine before men that they might see our good works and, acknowledging their intention and character, give glory and honor to God (Matt. 5:13–16). The Celtic Christians remind us that everything we do in culture must be undertaken self-consciously with a view to honoring God and declaring a worldview consistent with his rule and Word. In chapter 5 we shall see one recent and one contemporary Christian artist who show us how this prophetic role of culture can have powerful effects.

Culture matters, both to God and to his people. As our Celtic forebears remind us, we must not avoid the necessity of proclaiming our distinctly Christian message through all the vehicles of contemporary culture.

This, however, should not be taken to mean that all Christian culture is merely a subcategory of evangelism. There is much to be declared, for example, about the nature and purpose of human life under God and the meaning of things "under the heavens" that Christians can explore and express through their involvement in culture. Profound philosophical questions must be tackled; the joys and delights, as well as the trials and travails of the human situation must be examined; and the sheer beauty of the creation must be celebrated. But all of this should be done as part of a conscious effort to fulfill our callings as those sent to announce the coming and kingdom of him through whom all things are being reconciled back to God (2 Cor. 5:17–22). As Celtic Christian artists employed their culture to declare their faith in the all-integrating, all-ruling Son of God, so too we in the Christian community today must make certain both that we know the message of our faith and that we declare it clearly and consistently in all our cultural activities.

For the Christian who is becoming self-consciously involved in culture matters, the Celtic Christians invite us to embrace a wide range of cultural interests. At the same time, they warn us to filter all our cultural involvement through the grid of our Christian worldview and to direct our cultural work to embodying and proclaiming the same. Both Christians who work in the artistic arenas of culture and their fellows who participate with them in their own cultural spheres have a message to declare. We must guard against the dilution or compromise of that message by an unreflective, merely subjective approach to our involvement in culture matters.

Know your media

Second, the artists of the Celtic Christian period provide strong encouragement to today's Christians to know their media and strive for perfection in all aspects of cultural life. In the history of Christian art there is little to compare with Celtic ornamentation, illustration, and design as far as brilliance, exquisiteness of detail, consistency, and the combined beauty of the whole. These works reflect a devotion to excellence that can easily be overlooked in the drive to produce art quickly, inexpensively, and with a mass market in mind.

Much of the Christian culture that is available to the believing community today is at the level of crafts or popular entertainment, while the "common culture" expressed by most Christians in the ways they speak, work, and recreate shows little to distinguish it from the practice of their unbelieving neighbors. While more Christians are beginning to become involved in culture matters, there is little serious Christian art, either on exhibit or available for purchase. But this is not to say that no serious Christian art is being done. Rather, it is to acknowledge that the only Christian art in most homes consists of homemade or mass-produced plaques, ceramic items, various forms of tapestry (macramé, stitch-work, knitted items), ornamental Bible verses or inspirational quotes, or the increasingly ubiquitous works of Thomas Kinkade. Not much else in the way of Christian art finds its way into the service of the local church, either, where banners, clip-art, posters, decorative bulletin covers, and photographic collages are the most common artistic items. The names of serious Christian artists of the past are unknown to the vast majority of believers. And, while there is certainly a place for crafts in the Christian art endeavor, nevertheless, because of their sameness, accessibility to virtually anyone, regardless of level of real artistic ability (even this writer can paint by numbers), and essentially market-oriented nature, these cannot lead the way to renewal in serious Christian art or to a powerful role for culture in the mission of the church. Neither will they catalyze a Christian consensus on culture matters, encouraging loftier and more distinctly Christian expressions in conversation, relationships, and cultural engagement across the board.

Nor can Christians who are becoming involved in culture matters be satisfied with a kind of sanctified mediocrity. Serious, compelling, lasting art and culture takes time. It requires an understanding and mastery of media and techniques that only a few ever acquire. And it can, for those reasons, be somewhat expensive. Let those few creators among contemporary Christian artists, following the example of their Celtic forerunners, bravely resist the temptation to bypass excellence for the sake of marketability or mediocrity, and let them study ever to improve and perfect their God-given skills. And let the rest of us in the Christian community discover ways to encourage and support such makers of culture as they pursue their calling to serve the glory of God.

Adopt and adapt

Third, Celtic Christian artists provide an example of adopting and adapting that can serve contemporary Christians well.[26] Contemporary Christians cannot indulge the studied ignorance of cultural history that characterizes so many of their postmodern contemporaries.[27] Not only in art history in general, but particularly in the history of Christian culture, there are themes, techniques, and traditions to be understood and drawn on that can enrich the cultural work of this generation of Christians. Celtic artists did not need to deny their rich cultural heritage in order to produce a distinctively Christian artistic expression. Instead, they carefully adapted what had been handed down to them, making the rich heritage of Celtic art serve the purposes of the gospel in new and exciting ways.

There is a challenge here, not only to Christian artists, but to the rest of us as well, to become more familiar with and appreciative of the vast heritage of culture that has been produced by our forebears in the faith, whether in the arts and literature, social reform and renewal, or institutional innovation. As we should be able to see from this introductory examination of Celtic Christian art, there is much to learn and much from which we might benefit in our growth in and service to the Lord.

It is not necessary for contemporary Christian artists to despise all the forms of contemporary art, though they can be often confusing and sometimes disgusting. In certain ways, culture is what any generation decides it is. The various forms of postmodern art—the installation art of Bruce Naumann, the performance art of Sandra Bernhard, the photographic collages of Robert Rauschenberg, the free verse that fills the pages of *The American Poetry Review*, or the concept art of Christo, as well as such traditional, albeit greatly revised, forms as painting, printmaking, and sculpture—are all available to Christians for our distinctive cultural purposes.[28] The challenge to Christians involved in culture matters is to present their message with an awareness of contemporary forms and, where possible, by adapting these, not just rely on forms that Christians have always found familiar or consistent with their heritage.

The key to legitimizing contemporary forms will be in the unique ways that they are made to serve the gospel of Jesus Christ. Here, too, our Celtic forebears show the way, drawing as they did from forms, themes, and techniques of surrounding pagan cultures in order to enhance their own work and proclaim their distinctive message. They should encourage us to take something other than a merely dismissive or imitative approach to contemporary culture. Instead, we should study the various forms of contemporary culture, learn about the ways they are being used, and try to see how they might lend themselves to furthering our kingdom purposes in one way or another.

Communicate actively and clearly

Fourth, contemporary Christians can learn from their Celtic precursors how important for the success of their involvement in culture matters it can be to share, communicate, and collaborate, both with one another as well as the public they serve. It seems clear that Celtic artists worked together on many projects, sharing knowledge, insights, and skills in completely unselfish ways. It is significant that, apart from Eadfrith, the artist as well as the scribe of the Lindisfarne Gospels, the name of not a single Celtic artist has survived. Eadfrith's comes to us only by attribution from a later translator of the Lindisfarne Gospels. These artists seem never to have had a thought about personal gain or glory. By pooling their talents and carefully passing on what they had mastered, they hoped to produce a lasting art in all they did. In this they certainly succeeded. At the very least this suggests that Christians today should be talking and working together toward the achievement of some consensus on culture.

Moreover, Celtic Christian artists did not leave their public in the dark about the meaning of their art. Rather, their art became a focal point for teaching, evangelism, and worship, as artists and monks employed their creations to make plain the message that was so dear and urgent to them. Contemporary Christians must consider the implications of this twofold challenge to their own cultural endeavors, and whether more collaboration and interaction with one another as well as with the Christian community might not help to further their purposes.

Accept the challenge of innovation

Fifth, the accomplishment of Celtic Christian artists should encourage Christians today to be willing to innovate in their work, both in new cultural forms (illuminated manuscripts, carved crosses) and in new uses for existing forms (spirals, key-patterns, etc.). And those of us who are the "consumers" of the cultural creations of our Christian contemporaries must be open to learning about innovation and the new forms it creates.

Innovation can be easily stifled by closed-mindedness concerning forms or media, a market mentality, shortcuts that promote mediocrity, or a refusal to explain to colleagues, critics, and the public what is intended. But learning these lessons from our Celtic forebears can help contemporary Christians to make progress in this area as well. It will also go a long way toward helping the members of the Christian community understand the importance and value of culture in all its forms. This is an era in culture matters when innovation is very much prized, at least among secular critics. There is no reason why Christians should not be pointing the way to some new—or perhaps rediscovered—forms and expressions. We are already seeing innovation—some might say too much innovation—in Christian music and liturgy. Also, Christian educators, realizing the need to create new forms for the transmission of the biblical worldview, have begun to pioneer new approaches to training children, church leaders, and even pastors and theologians. There is no reason not to encourage innovation on the part of informed Christians across the board in culture matters.

The role of the church in culture matters

Sixth, the Celtic Christians remind us that the church can and should take an active role in culture matters.[29] Churches and their leaders have always been significantly involved in culture matters—creating new institutions, sponsoring artists and exhibiting their works, supporting education and social welfare, and exercising vigilance over potentially harmful cultural elements and trends. The Celtic churches were no different. Indeed, there is very much a sense in which the Celtic expression of "church" itself became a unique, albeit temporary cultural form. The *paruchia* (family) model used to establish, preserve, and advance particular monastic traditions provided forms of worship, rules of discipline, guidelines for penance, and a wide range of cultural forms that helped to create identity, meaning, and purpose that spanned many generations.

Many churches today have already begun to demonstrate a commitment to culture matters, in their support of educational institutions and mission endeavors, their use of "new songs" in worship, and their involvement with the Internet and various forms of local and on-demand publishing. Our Celtic forebears in the faith would salute such involvement.

Serve the community

Finally, contemporary Christians, in their use of all forms of culture, can learn from the artists of the Celtic period to serve the needs of their community, and not merely their own personal vision or aspirations. As culture is a gift from God, like all of his good gifts it must be used for his glory in loving service to others (James 1:17; 1 Cor.12:7–11). There would seem to be little room in any endeavor of Christian culture for a merely personal vision, that is, one that serves only as an outlet for the individual's interests or expressiveness. While all culture must include this, lasting culture will also speak to the needs and interests of the community. This was certainly the case with Celtic Christian artists.

From their example Christians today might begin to prosper by considering more carefully the needs of the Christian community for such things as everyday art (fashion, jewelry), domestic art, educational art, and liturgical and devotional art, as well as art to encourage intellectual stimulation, social cohesiveness, and works of ministry. The Christian public's readiness to accept crafts and mass-produced art in all these areas would seem to indicate an openness on its part to more serious products, that is, cultural creations that are the work of particular craftspeople or schools and reflect the carefulness of taste, design, and execution that are the hallmarks of true art. This aspect of Celtic Christian art should also lead us to reflect more carefully on our use of such everyday cultural forms as conversation (including email), dress and manners, and ongoing personal development. In a day when deconstructionism, postmodernism, and widespread libertinism have undermined language, civility, tradition, and intellectual and spiritual development, Christians can begin to assert an altogether new and fresh presence in all these areas and more by pursuing a vision of culture matters that expresses love for God and man in compelling ways.

We in the Christian community should be encouraged by the growing interest and work in the various fields of endeavor that are beginning to appear from within the ranks of the evangelical Christian community. It is a healthy sign that the community is beginning to think seriously about the application of our faith to areas of culture and society that have for too long been ignored. Each member of the Christian community should welcome the work of Christian artists and seek to encourage them in their important endeavor. We must become more knowledgeable about culture matters, and more willing to understand and receive the work of culture creators in our midst. And we must take more seriously our own involvement in culture matters as an important part of advancing the reign of righteousness, peace, and joy in the Holy Spirit that is the kingdom of God (Rom. 14:17).

For their part, Christians who are creating culture have a responsibility to make sure that the culture they produce is consistent with the calling they have embraced, the traditions they have inherited, and the needs and mission of the community they represent. To this end they have much to gain from a study of the Christian artists of previous generations, in particular, the Christian artists who produced the various works of the Celtic Christian period.

Contemporary Exemplar: An Interview with Phil Keaggy

One contemporary Christian artist who embodies many of the lessons of Celtic Christian art is guitarist and lyricist Phil Keaggy. Keaggy has been hailed as one of the greatest living guitarists. His instrumentals and vocals draw on a great many influences—of culture, period, genre, and style—but his message is consistent and clear: Music is a gift from God, who fills our lives with wonder and joy, and who alone deserves the praise for every good gift. By his own admission, Keaggy is not exactly a "household name" among contemporary Christians. You won't hear his cuts on many contemporary Christian music stations. His music is at times complex, but always thoughtful, rich in sources, and filled with the grace and truth of his profound Christian faith. He borrows from many traditions—ancient, pop, jazz, Latin, classical, and liturgical—to package a message rooted in God's goodness and grace and calling listeners to a deeper experience of eternal truths.

In a 2001 interview with Phil Keaggy, I chatted with him about his views of the role of music in human life, and its ability to nurture the affections. Excerpts from that interview follow, and they reflect the kind of approach to culture matters that mirrors the experience of Celtic Christian artists and can contribute toward a genuine Christian consensus.[30]

Let's talk a little about some of your music. What are you trying to get your music to do? What should it do for people? How should it affect them?

Well, there are two sides to my creativity in music, the vocal side and the instrumental side. It's interesting—I did an album recently called "Inseparable," which I did basically for myself, like a piece of marble I had to sculpt for no else but me. As the album took shape I realized this was not a happy, bouncy album. It addresses areas where people hurt, and when it came out, I started getting letters from people telling me how much the album had meant to them, how it had touched them deeply, given them hope and encouragement, and reminded them of God's love in special ways. They felt like I knew what they were going through and cared—even though only God knows the details of their lives. If I have the Spirit of Christ, then I can create things that will resonate with people's hearts. Because we're all part of each other in the Body of Christ, we don't know all the details of other people's hurts, but God does, and he can use us in surprising ways to minister his grace to people we've never met. So this album—although it was not well received by the industry or the listening public—has reached a few people in very deep ways, providing comfort and encouragement at just the right time. That means the world to me.

On the instrumental side I've had people say about my music that, although there were no words, something about the melodies and rhythms really touched them. So what I'm trying to do with my music is give people an opportunity to hear and see with the heart, music that can enhance and bless their lives, adding joy, beauty, and hope at just the right time.

And I would say of your music, at least my experience of it, it tends to tap into some affections that I don't normally experience—wonder, majesty, pain—and teaches me how to feel those things. This is really important to me, because as I exercise those affections listening to your music I find they are more readily available to me in other areas of my life—when I come into the presence of God's glory, when I'm worshipping him, or when I'm called on to minister to someone in some new or unexpected way.

That's what it does for you?

Yes, exactly.

That says it much better than I could, but I think it's what I'm trying to do. I've found sometimes, especially when I've been listening to a CD of old Irish tunes, that something in me is stirred and deeply affected. I wonder sometimes if there might not be something genetic about memory that accounts for how these feelings persist generation after generation. At any rate, music certainly taps those feelings better than anything else I know.

I know that some poets, as they are writing their verse, are thinking to themselves, "What do I want the reader to see as he or she reads this? What vision or insight am I trying to get across?" Do you ever think about your music that way?

Yes, I think I would like that to happen. For instance, on the *Cinemascapes* album there is a piece called "A Mother's Son," and it has an Irish flavor to it. The music of that piece spoke to me about a mother's love for her son, and I couldn't help but think about a mother sending her son off to war in another land, and how her heart goes with him. A song like this can possibly encourage people to think about their relationships with others: Are they what they ought to be, or could be? I wrote a tune called "Under the Grace" for two important people in my life, Jesus and my wife, Bernadette. It's about sacrificial love, love that is willing to give up everything for the beloved. And then I heard that song in a different context, in which a friend had lost his wife, and it took on a deeper meaning for me. I began to feel an emotion that I didn't feel when I originally wrote the song. The song took on a different perspective and deeper meaning when I heard it in a context of someone else's loss.

*I'll tell you what got me started thinking about this notion of
"seeing with eyes of music." The song "A Little Bit of Light": As I
listened to this it was clear that you were singing about Vincent Van
Gogh, and I couldn't help but think about Don MacLean's "Vincent."
His is a sad and tragic song, yet yours is not in the least sad or tragic.
You seemed to be saying to me, "Look at Vincent this way. Sure he
had some dark paintings and a sad life, but look at the whole of it,
see the beautiful colors and persistent points of light, and you'll see
that this man had a different view of life than you might have previously thought." I don't know that many people today think of Van
Gogh in this way.*

Neither did the religious leaders of his time, who, as you know,
rejected him as an evangelist, which is all he ever wanted to be. He
just wanted to serve the Lord, to care for his fellow man, and he had
an artistic and giving heart. I read a wonderful book about Vincent
that focused on his spirituality, and that helped me to have a new
appreciation of him. Keith Moore wrote the lyrics to this song, and
I wrote the music, and we both put it on albums. Then this young
girl in Canada, Sarah Mainland, wrote Keith a letter and said she is
a blind guitarist and loves this song so much. She said that one day
Jesus was going to allow her to see everything in its grand beauty,
and she wanted to know if we could help her learn the song. So I
made a CD—about 20 minutes or so—and helped her learn how to
sing it. She learned it and sent me back a letter in Braille, with her
mother's translation below the Braille. I have it here. She writes,
"Thank you so much for taking the time out of your busy day to
put together the song 'A Little Bit of Light.' When I have learned it
I'll send you a tape of it." And they sent me a coffee cup with my
name in Braille on it. So here's a song that touched deeply a young
girl who can't even see.

*I'm sure you've noticed that, in that song, both the lowest and
highest points in the melodic range carry the phrase, "a little bit of
light." You seem to be saying that light from the Lord is the high
point of our experience, but it's also with us even in our dark nights
of the soul.*

That's right, you're right!

*Phil, I also want to ask you about "Tender Love." Now this is
deliberately Beatle-esque.*

Yes it is. When the first Beatles anthology came out, with "Free
as a Bird" on it, I just loved that song. I watched the program, went

right downstairs to my studio, and wrote the song, including all the parts. It was just suddenly, completely there. So it was a deliberately Beatles-influenced piece. Just as the Beatles borrowed from influences like Bach, I have been influenced by them, as well as many others.

When you do this, is this just at attempt to show appreciation for the Beatles, or are you trying, as the Apostle Paul might say, to "take captive" the forms and style of the Beatles to make them serve your music and message? Or do you just like the way it sounds?

I think it's kind of a natural flow that happens. I don't really think about whether I'm honoring the Beatles, or might reach their audience with my words. I don't really think like that. It's more, "Wow, this feels good. I'm going to wear this." This comes naturally to me, and I'm just doing it to express myself. I've not been, compared to many others, a very commercially successful artist—of course, I do make a living from it, but I'm not exactly a household name. I try to write what I'm feeling at any moment, depending on whatever may be influencing me at the time. "Tender Love" came out of an experience like that.

I think this is one of the things I especially appreciate about your music, that it's not formulaic. You are very unpredictable. So much contemporary Christian music seems to me to be stuck in the worn-out forms of rock music, with little in the way of originality or innovation. The genius of music over the years has been to try to say, How can we broaden the horizons of music, stretch out its line a little further? And people who do that, like, for example, Bach, aren't always appreciated in their day. I'm hopeful that a day will come when people will begin to see that what you are doing in your music is pointing in some new directions, stretching out the forms of Christian music and challenging us to listen more carefully and think differently about what music is and what it can do.

I would love to be able to do that, and that's exactly what keeps me going. I want to know God's new mercies and unfailing compassion every morning, and the gift of creativity is part of that. As I tap into God and his vast resources, I hope he'll give me the ability to spread his grace to others through my music.

Questions for Study or Discussion

1. In what ways—art, music, poetry, liturgy—have you experienced the influence of Celtic Christian art? What kinds of

affections does that art stir within you? How does it make you feel? What do you think about when you are in the presence of these Celtic Christian influences?

2. As you read this chapter, did you find your interest in Celtic Christian art piqued? In what ways? Why do you think that Celtic Christian art has had such enduring appeal over the years?

3. Review the lessons that we may gain from the Celtic Christian approach to culture matters. Which of them seem most pertinent to your own involvement in culture? Why?

4. Listen to an album by Phil Keaggy. Do you agree that his music differs from much of contemporary Christian music? What kind of influences can you detect in his music? How would you summarize his message? Which of the seven lessons of Celtic Christian art does Keaggy seem to embody?

5. Review the goals you set for your study of culture matters. Do you want to change or clarify those in any way? Are you making any progress toward them?

Education for Cultural Renewal

Calvin, Geneva, and Educational Innovation

Pedagogy was the key to the Calvinist enterprise. The catechism, preaching, and the admonitions of the consistory had no other end but to profoundly transform mentalities by sowing the good seed of the gospel in men's hearts.

Bernard Cottret

But that is not the way you learned Christ!—assuming that you have heard about him and were taught in him, as the truth is in Jesus, to put off your old self, which belongs to your former manner of life and is corrupt through deceitful desires, and to be renewed in the spirit of your minds, and to put on the new self, created after the likeness of God in true righteousness and holiness.

Ephesians 4:20–24

A GENUINE CONSENSUS ON culture matters among members of the Christian community must involve an ongoing critique of contemporary culture and fervent devotion to the work of forging altogether new forms of culture. The kind of penetrating critique offered by Augustine and the unique cultural form that flourished among the Christians of the Celtic period do not simply happen; they are the result of thoughtful reflection and diligent teaching and learning that takes the whole counsel of God seriously for every area of human life and interest, including the work of culture. Augustine and the Celtic Christians understood this and made the work of education a central aspect of their missions. Achieving consensus on culture matters today will require an equally energetic effort in the area of education. The churches are not wanting of abundant and varied educational opportunities; yet the members of the Christian community need to consider whether the program of Christian formation we are currently pursuing will be sufficient to equip the saints for renewal in culture matters. The present fragmented state of the Christian consensus on culture suggests that something is amiss in the education we are providing the saints for this important part of their callings.

The Christian enterprise has always been characterized by a strong emphasis on education. From the earliest days of the church, preaching, teaching, catechizing, specific kinds of training for ministry, and the pursuit of more general studies have been part of the Christian project to bring the gospel of Jesus Christ to bear on every aspect of human life and interest. Looking to Jesus as the "Master Teacher," Christians through the centuries have sought for relevant and effective ways to communicate the unchanging truths of the gospel amid the changing tides of time and culture. Over the years Christians have pioneered educational breakthroughs, many of which continue in one form or another to this day: the work of catechesis; pastoral and missionary education; the publication of Bibles and other Christian literature; the creation of statewide school systems, as under Alcuin in the empire of Charlemagne, Luther in sixteenth-century Germany, or Roman Catholicism in this country; the development of the modern university during the medieval scholastic period; the Sunday school movement, begun in nineteenth-century England; and the day school and home school efforts of recent years in America.

The church in post–World War II America experienced a flourishing of Christian educational activity such as has perhaps never before been seen in Christian history. The past two generations in America have witnessed the development and widespread deployment of more educational institutions, programs, media, and material in the service of the gospel than in any previous period of church history. Today, in early twenty-first-century America, the Christian community boasts more Sunday schools, private schools, Bible study groups, colleges and seminaries, workshops and seminars, radio and television programming, and other assorted educational vehicles and media, as well as people and resources invested in operating these enterprises, than has ever been seen in Christian history. There are more Christian educators, facilities, books, audio and video resources, and other aids to instruction than ever, and more people are sitting in classes, signing up for seminars, enrolling in courses of study, reading Christian literature, receiving diplomas and degrees from Christian institutions, and listening to Christian programming than in any previous period.

Yet for all this, something seems to be terribly wrong with the work of Christian education today. For when it comes to culture matters, and the kind of culture that guides and expresses the peculiar convictions of this generation, believers in Christ continue to be divided in their approach. Moreover, the Christian community as a whole, in spite of recent high visibility in the political arena, is plainly on the margin of cultural influence. In the American church we are awash in teaching but show little evidence of having learned much that is distinctly Christian with respect to culture matters. We are not "learning Christ," as Paul put it, in the kind of transformational way that has allowed the church to exercise much of a formative role in developing uniquely Christian forms of culture, or in shaping the values and culture of the society in which we exist. We seem, to borrow another Pauline notion, to be "always learning and never able to arrive at a knowledge of the truth" (2 Tim. 3:7). The church has become ingrown and methodical, and appears to be confused over the true nature of discipleship.[1] We need Christian education that emphasizes "the cost of discipleship, the absolute claim of God over our entire life, the necessity of a faith that issues forth in obedience, and our belonging to an alternative culture shaped by the kingdom of Jesus."[2] As Craig Dykstra puts it,

> Christian educators need to think about how to lead people beyond a reliance on "random acts of kindness" into shared patterns of life that are informed by the deepest insights of our traditions, and about how to lead people beyond privatized spiritualities into more thoughtful participation in God's activity in the world.[3]

What we need, he continues, is a kind of Christian education that promotes "participation in the educating work of God's Spirit among us and within us."[4]

If we are ever going to realize a renewed consensus on culture matters, or be able to shape the culture around us more than we are shaped by it, we will need to review the work of our Christian educational enterprises in order to discover what is amiss in all this frenzy of activity; then we will need to take up new endeavors, target new objectives, focus on new subjects, and employ new media and means toward the end of realizing the kingdom of God in culture matters. And in this undertaking it can be useful to look back to previous periods of Christian history in order to discover what we might learn from those whose work in Christian education did manage to accomplish long-term, lasting change. One such individual was John Calvin, the sixteenth-century Geneva Reformer.

In this chapter we will look to Calvin's writings and ministry in order to see how he conceived the work of Christian education, and to consider his contribution to Christian education in his generation. Calvin implemented a dramatic and comprehensive program of education in Geneva that reached all the population and worked to promote seeking the kingdom of God and his righteousness as of primary importance. His was a work of education for spiritual and cultural renewal. We will also examine Calvin's theory of learning, for it is in this area especially that the church today would seem to have much to gain by reviewing the work of the Geneva Reformer.[5]

Calvin on the Purpose of Christian Education

In Christian educational circles today it is impossible not to see the emphasis that is placed on meeting the felt needs of learners. Indeed, church leaders go to great lengths to try to discover the needs of their members and to develop curricula, training, and resources designed to address those needs. One cannot escape the sense that Christian education in contemporary American churches is decidedly person-centered in its orientation and execution. John Calvin would have raised a skeptical eyebrow at such an approach to teaching the saints of God. In his "never-ceasing search for the renovation of the contemporary educational system,"[6] Calvin pursued loftier objectives through a comprehensive program of educational innovation and reform. For Calvin the purpose of education was to ground the Christian population in the teaching of God's Word. To that end he pioneered a program that was targeted at individual, social, and cultural renewal. Four characteristics in particular distinguished Calvin's work in the arena of education: the primacy of the Word of God, the development of a comprehensive program of instruction, training that focused on renewal in the kingdom of God, and the continuous oversight of all educational work by the church.

The primacy of the Word

Calvin held that "the only due method of teaching in the Church is according to the prescription and rule of his word,"[7] that is, the Word of God in scripture. He insisted that it is through the scriptures that we learn to "worship [God] with perfect integrity of heart and unfeigned obedience, and also to depend entirely upon his goodness."[8] He believed that the scriptures were absolutely indispensable to the development of Christian faith and conduct, not only for the life of the individual believer, but for all corporate expressions of Christian conduct and culture as well. He wrote in 1550 to a new believer, encouraging him to take up the daily exercise of reading and reflecting on scripture: "For if you make a constant study of the word of the Lord, you will be quite able to guide your life to the highest excellence."[9] Calvin sought to have all aspects of life in Geneva regularly scrutinized by the Word of God and reformed according to its teachings. As the introduction to the *Ecclesiastical Ordinances* of 1541 states so clearly, "it has seemed to us advisable that the spiritual government of the kind which our Lord demonstrated and instituted by His Word should be set out in good order so that it may be established and observed among us."[10] For Calvin it was more important to answer the question, How faithfully does our system of life, government, and ministry conform to the criteria of scripture? than to settle for such lesser criteria as the communication of tradition, learner satisfaction, convenience, or expediency. Calvin knew that if real renewal was to occur, both in the hearts of God's people and the culture in which they lived, the scriptures would have to become more central and vital in the experience of every citizen.

For Calvin, teaching was the primary means of setting forth the unadulterated truth of God's Word, which alone could accomplish reformation in church and culture. As Ronald Wallace has observed, "What Calvin lived to achieve in Geneva deserves to be called a commonwealth in which both Church and State serve each other in serving the Word of God, and the individual is nurtured and trained to true freedom and responsibility in the community."[11] For the people of sixteenth-century Geneva, this represented a decidedly new focus; indeed, Calvin brought a veritable revolution to Geneva with his conviction that the people should be taught by every means not merely to adhere to the strict teachings and protocols of the church, but to seek the knowledge of God, so that they might live for his glory. Wallace explained concerning Calvin's emphasis on the Word of God,

> The light of the Gospel must be allowed constantly to shine from the Church into the surrounding community in order to help the whole of humanity find the best directions and limitations for its self-development in personal, family, social and cultural life, and to come to a true understanding of itself.[12]

Calvin insisted on the importance of the people of Geneva hearing, understanding, and obeying the saving and transforming message of Christ in the scriptures. The whole of his theological and ecclesiastical undertaking in Geneva was conceived in this manner.

A comprehensive program

Education in the early sixteenth century was, for the most part, still following the models inherited from the reforms of previous centuries. The work of teaching was largely in the hands of the church, reserved only for a select few, and devoted to turning out graduates who could fill vacancies in the ranks of the priesthood, civil service, law, and teaching. The purpose of this educational program, assumed more than stated, was to perpetuate the social structures of the late medieval period: professional castes of priests, rulers, and lawyers maintaining a defined order in which an emerging middle class could produce wealth, while the peasants would have to be content with remaining bound to poverty and the soil.

In 1541, upon his return to Geneva from three years of exile, John Calvin took up afresh the radical agenda that had been, in part, responsible for his expulsion from that city. A major feature of that agenda was a comprehensive program of education for the Genevan people. Little in the way of formal education existed in Geneva in 1541, and what was available "was neither highly valued nor highly paid in the materialistic and dissolute city of Geneva."[13] Over the next twenty years Calvin introduced and oversaw a program of instruction designed to bring every citizen of Geneva and its environs under the tutelage of scripture and right doctrine. Starting from nothing, he set forth a comprehensive educational plan, then steadily worked to bring together the resources and people needed to ensure faithful instruction of children and adults for deeper spiritual living and a wide range of callings. His program involved the creation of new schools, the reform and expansion of instructional media, and the increase of preaching and teaching for all members of the community. His objective was nothing less than a program of universal Christian education, and he determined to employ every means possible to achieve this end.

In the course of time the pastors of Geneva, under Calvin's leadership, established and maintained not only a thriving ministry of education within the churches, but also a model system of schools for boys, girls, and higher-level students. In the churches, instruction was carried out through preaching and catechism. Preaching was frequent, as many as three times on Sundays, and on Monday, Wednesday, and Friday during the week. The catechism was taught in special classes on Sundays at noon. Although Calvin prepared the catechism primarily for use with children, some adults apparently attended these instructional periods as well. Instruction in the catechism was in the hands of the teachers, accompanied by other young men specially trained for this activity.[14] The end of the work of catechesis was that children might be prepared to make a personal, credible, and public profession of their faith in Christ.

Adding to his work of preaching and catechism, Calvin led the way in establishing three different schools in Geneva. Of the school for girls, not much is known, save that it was maintained separately from that for the boys. The boys' school was intended as a preparatory school for university. Here the boys studied languages, the classics, and philosophy. At the university they took up the study of theology, the sciences, and mathematics. After Calvin's death, medicine and law were added to the curriculum. The primary purpose of the university was practical: to prepare young men for the ministry and for civil service unto the glory of God and the edification of his church.

Calvin's program may not strike us as particularly daring, but for his day it was truly radical, not only in scope but in format. This comprehensive attempt to bring the instruction of God's Word to all the people of Geneva paralleled developments to the north, where Luther and Melanchthon were pioneering an educational reformation of their own, and in Strasbourg, where Martin Bucer had introduced Calvin to the importance of such a program. Education in Geneva, though it depended primarily on the work of pastors and teachers, also involved parents and civil magistrates in appropriate oversight roles. It was a program of universal education designed to fit the people of God for kingdom living in a changing world. People were expected to attend the instruction appropriate to them, and pastors and teachers were regularly reviewed in their preaching and teaching. Calvin understood that seeking the kingdom of God required all the people of Geneva to come under the authority of God's Word, and all those involved in the work of education to pursue excellence in their callings. Regular visitations of the churches of Geneva by the pastors, together with the careful exercise of church discipline, were employed to ensure that the people of Geneva took the Word of God to heart. Calvin's innovative approach to the scope, content, and results of the educational work of the church should challenge contemporary Christians to careful consideration of our own efforts in this vein.

Education for renewal

Calvin testified to having three specific purposes in mind for the course of his ministry in all its expressions: "how the glory of God is to be maintained on earth inviolate, how the truth of God is to preserve its dignity, how the kingdom of Christ is to continue among us compact and secure."[15] As Stanford Reid summarizes Calvin's educational agenda, "one might say that the basic objective which he had in mind was the inculcation of the knowledge of God and His works, for Christian service."[16] Calvin's preaching, teaching, and other work were undertaken to prepare people for the task of advancing the kingdom of Christ in every area of life. The church would teach, and the people were expected to respond with obedience reaching to every aspect of their daily lives. His focus was not, in the first instance, on them and their needs—which, in a city periodically beset by enemies, plague, and heresy, and trying to navigate the uncertain waters of reformation, would have been many—but on God, his Word, and the purposes of his kingdom. In the educational program developed under Calvin, the people of Geneva were taught to understand and embrace the *will* of God in the *knowledge* of God for the sake of the *kingdom* of God. Thus, Calvin's pastoral and educational work had an *objective focus* (the will of God in scripture), was directed at *personal application* (the knowledge of God that leads to eternal life), and sought broad *cultural impact* (as the kingdom of

God unfolded throughout the city). As Ronald Wallace summarizes Calvin's educational purpose,

> The individual must respond to the approach and concern of the community and gladly fulfill his vocation within it. Whatever his work he is to try to see it as a sacred calling, and through doing it he will be helped to find and fulfill the will of God.[17]

Calvin's program was designed to promote spiritual and cultural renewal throughout the city. He labored to inculcate a biblical worldview that would promote and sustain reformation in every area of life.

Calvin viewed all his work of preaching and teaching, and all the other educational works that he inaugurated in Geneva, as means to edifying the church and glorifying God through the exposition of his truth, so that the people of Geneva might know the Lord and worship and serve him appropriately. Unlike many Christian educators today, Calvin would not say that he had succeeded when the people of Geneva were *happy*, but when they and their culture were *holy to the Lord*.

Oversight by the church

Consistent with his overall purpose, Calvin looked to the scriptures for guidance in how to arrange the work of teaching and learning in Geneva. He believed that the churches of Geneva, under the leadership of the pastors of the city, and in communication with civil authorities, should be responsible for carrying out this work. The reformation in Geneva would be accomplished in no "other way than by the education of the Church."[18] Both the civil magistrate and the home were to have a role in the work of education, but it was primarily through the churches, overseen by their pastors, meeting as a consistory, that this task was to be accomplished.

His reading of the scriptures led Calvin to conclude that the church—as embodied in its pastors—must take the lead in the work of reformation.[19] Parents would certainly have a role to play,[20] as would the civil authorities.[21] But the primary responsibility for the work of reformation, including that of Christian education, was lodged in the church, in her pastors and officers.

In his program instructional responsibilities were divided between pastors and teachers.[22] Calvin thought it important to maintain a clear distinction between these offices. Both ministers and teachers were called

to their tasks by the church and were to be adequately provided for in
their temporal needs by the people they served. The function of the pastor was

> feeding the sheep of Jesus Christ on the one hand with instruction,
> admonition, consolation, exhortation, deprecation; and on the other
> resisting all false doctrines and deceptions of the devil, without
> mixing with the pure doctrines of Scripture their dreams or foolish
> imaginings.[23]

Teachers, on the other hand, were responsible only for "the instruction of the faithful in true doctrine."[24] Teachers functioned both
in the churches of Geneva and in the college founded there. In the
former they gave primary attention to teaching theology from both
the Old and New Testaments.[25] They also instructed in languages and
humanities with a view to preparing at least some of the students
either for ministry or for civil service.[26] Both teachers and pastors
were accountable for their work to the company of pastors of the
city, who regularly reviewed their work and made suggestions and
changes as needed.[27] Thus, the Church of Geneva, through its officers, and under the oversight of the company of pastors, took direct
responsibility for developing, conducting, assessing, and revising the
work of education throughout the city.

Calvin's Theory of Learning

To this point we have been retracing a rather well-worn path. However, when we turn to consider aspects of Calvin's theory of learning,
we strike out in something of a new direction. Calvin believed that
learning is an inherently human activity, that true learning is a work
of the Holy Spirit leading to growth in the knowledge of God, and
that achieving that end lays certain crucial responsibilities on those
who learn and those who teach.

People inherently learners

Calvin viewed human beings as inherently learning creatures.[28] We
cannot help but learn about God, since God has deposited in the souls
of people a "seed of religion" and continually manifests himself to
them "in the whole structure of the created universe"[29] and, beyond

that, in the scriptures. People are bound to learn about God as a simple matter of existence, from the "most illiterate peasant" to the most accomplished student of liberal studies.[30] Yet not all learn about God in the same manner. Some deny the knowledge of God. Those, on the other hand, who apply themselves unto the knowledge of God are gripped in their hearts and minds (affect and cognition) and show the fruit of their learning in reformed lives (practice).[31] Such learning, however, is not the product of mere intellectual activity, be it ever so frequent, willful, or diligent; rather, it is an inward work of the Holy Spirit in the souls and lives of those who desire to know God:

> the testimony of the Spirit is superior to reason, for as God alone can properly bear witness to his own words, so these words will not obtain full credit in the hearts of men, until they are sealed by the inward testimony of the Spirit. The same Spirit, therefore, who spoke by the mouth of the prophets, must penetrate our hearts, in order to convince us that they faithfully deliver the message with which they were divinely entrusted.[32]

True learning, therefore, is consummately a work of the Holy Spirit. He alone leads learners into the true knowledge of the living God, and all that pertains thereunto for daily living. Only teaching that proceeds according to the ends of the Spirit, therefore, can expect to contribute to the kind of learning that results in personal and cultural renewal in the knowledge of God. To have the benefit of the blessing and power of the Spirit, therefore, Christian teaching must aim at the advance of Christ's Kingdom and his righteousness as its first priority. It must work to lead learners to seek and know the Lord for the whole of life.

The end of learning

But what does it mean to "know" God?

> By the knowledge of God, I understand that by which we not only conceive that there is some God, but also apprehend what it is for our interest, and conducive to his glory, what, in short, it is befitting to know concerning him. For, properly speaking, we cannot say that God is known where there is no religion or piety.[33]

Thus, to "know God" involves both the acquisition of certain factual data about him, and application of that information in our individual lives, so as to nurture true religious experience and to fit one for life in the kingdom. Learning, as Calvin approached the task, involves both content and application, mind and heart, soul and life. Further, learning that leads to the knowledge of God must concentrate on a twofold focus, involving our experience of God as Creator as well as Redeemer.[34] With respect to the former,

> we must be so persuaded not only that as he once formed the world, so he now sustains it by his boundless power, governs it by his wisdom, preserves it by his goodness, in particular, rules the human race with justice and judgment, bears with them in mercy, shields them by his protection; but also that not a particle of light, or wisdom, or justice, or power, or rectitude, or genuine truth, will anywhere be found, which does not flow from him, and of which he is not the cause; in this way we must learn to expect and ask all things from him, and thankfully ascribe to him whatever we receive.[35]

That is, the knowledge of God as Creator leads learners to look entirely toward him, to depend on him for all things, and to orient the entirety of their lives toward serving him. He is to be related to as the focal point for every aspect of life and interest, since he is the Source from which all of life derives and the Means by which it all is sustained. To know God as Creator, in short, is to acquiesce in his sovereignty for the whole of our lives. This was not a view of learning that would be content merely to transfer information from a teacher's notes to those of a student, to achieve high marks on an exam, to nurture a narrow sense of spiritual well-being, or to earn a certificate or degree. This was learning for personal and cultural renewal.

The knowledge of God as Redeemer, Calvin believed, is experienced through faith in Jesus Christ[36] and induces people to the true worship of God and confidence in the hope of everlasting life.[37] Overall, therefore, we may conclude that, as Calvin understood the end of learning, an individual has truly learned only when he or she has come, through faith in Jesus Christ, to reverence and fear God, to anticipate and work for his blessings in every area of life, to serve him entirely in the progress of his kingdom, and to thank and glorify him for the benefits received.[38] And, as we have noted, this involves a surrendering of the whole person—soul and body—so that a complete transformation occurs.

The knowledge of God thus entered into immediately has the effect of turning a person's attention to himself.[39] As learners see themselves as beings before God their Creator and Redeemer, they also begin to understand and embrace what it is proper for them to consider with respect to themselves:

> in considering the knowledge which man ought to have of himself, it seems quite proper to divide it thus, *first,* to consider the end for which he was created, and qualities—by no means contemptible qualities—with which he was endued, thus urging him to meditate on divine worship and the future life; and, *secondly,* to consider his faculties, or rather want of faculties—a want which, when perceived, will annihilate all his confidence, and cover him with confusion. The tendency of the former view is to teach him what his duty is, of the latter, to make him aware of how far he is able to perform it.[40]

This, then, is the other side of the learning-process coin. As people increasingly concentrate on their lives as image-bearers of God, they come to strive after a clear intellect, self-control over their affections—"all his senses duly regulated"—and a walk of gratitude and obedience before their sovereign Lord.[41] By the right use of intellect people learn "to distinguish between objects, according as they seem deserving of being approved or disapproved."[42] By the proper exercise of their wills they learn "to choose and follow what the intellect declares to be good, to reject and shun what it declares to be bad."[43] They cannot be said to be truly learning whose study of God and contemplation of themselves do not produce evidence of a lively faith: "if the knowledge of God, in so far as it fails to produce this effect, is fleeting and vain, it is clear that all those who do not direct the whole thoughts and actions of their lives to this end fail to fulfill the law of their being."[44]

Thus, in matters both of the knowledge of God and of themselves, Calvin sought a quality of learning that involved a radical reorienting of an individual's entire lifestyle, one that would draw him or her into a deeper and more personally comprehensive dependence upon God. Ultimately this is a work that only the Holy Spirit can accomplish[45]; yet Calvin acknowledged that both the learners and the teachers had significant roles and duties to fulfill in order that true learning might ensue.

Duties of learners

In order to achieve the quality of learning Calvin sought to bring about, the learners had to engage themselves in the fulfillment of three primary

responsibilities. First among these was faithful and active attendance at
public assemblies for instruction:

> Pride, or fastidiousness, or emulation, induces many to persuade
> themselves that they can profit sufficiently by reading and meditating
> in private, and thus to despise public meetings and deem preaching
> superfluous. But since as much as in them lies they lose or burst the
> sacred bond of unity, none of them escapes the just punishment of this
> impious divorce, but become fascinated with pestiferous errors, and the
> foulest delusions. Wherefore, in order that the pure simplicity of the
> faith may flourish among us, let us not decline to use this exercise of
> piety, which God by his institution of it has shown to be necessary.[46]

Genevans were to enter with seriousness of heart and mind into
worship and instruction, and this, presumably, throughout the entire
course of their lives. This corresponds well with Calvin's high view
of the teaching ministry as the primary means unto the reformation
of the church: "As we receive the true ministers of the Word of God
as messengers and ambassadors of God, it is necessary to listen to
them as to himself, as we hold their ministry to be a commission from
God necessary in the church."[47]

This commitment to active participation was to be impressed upon
the learners from the very youngest age. The habit of learning would
be inculcated in the young through their participation in Sunday catechism,[48] wherein understanding the nature and importance of true learning was made an integral part of what would eventually become their
public profession of faith in Christ.[49] Consider the following prescribed
response for the catechists concerning their response to God's Word:

> If we lay hold on it with complete heartfelt conviction as nothing less
> than truth come down from heaven; if we show ourselves docile to it; if we
> subdue our wills and minds to his obedience; if we love it heartily; if
> having it once engraved on our hearts and its roots fixed there, so that
> it bring forth fruit in our lives; if finally we be formed to its rule—then
> it will turn to our salvation, as intended.[50]

Calvin was emphatic about the citizenry's need for the learning that
could come about only through involvement in public instruction:

> the Church can only be edified by external preaching, and there is no
> other bond by which saints can be kept together than by uniting with

one consent to observe the order which God has appointed in his Church for learning and making progress.[51]

As a corollary, he warned that "all who reject the spiritual food of the soul divinely offered to them by the hands of the Church, deserve to perish of hunger and famine."[52]

Second, as diligent as they were to be concerning their attendance at public meetings of instruction, learners were to be equally diligent over their personal study of the scriptures. This, too, was to be part of their earliest training in Christian instruction. Masters (the teachers) were bound to ask of their catechists,

M: But are we not to apply diligence and strive with all zeal to advance in [Scripture] by reading, hearing, and meditating?

C: Certainly, while everyone ought to exercise himself in daily reading, at the same time also all are to attend with special regularity the gatherings where the doctrine of salvation is expounded in the company of the faithful.[53]

Everyone was to apply himself to becoming a "disciple of Scripture."[54] Yet, since this discipline, if carried out in solitude, could lead to all manner of false interpretations and heresy, it was to be consistently balanced by participation in public instruction, as we have seen.

Finally, it was every learner's duty to exercise vigilance over his or her own life, so that the learning gained in public and private might come to fruition in full and perfect obedience to the Lord: "For not only does faith, full and perfect faith, but all correct knowledge of God, originate in obedience."[55] Learning was not complete, and learners were not to be satisfied with their studies, until improvement in their lives was evident, and that throughout the course of their lives.

Duties of instructors

On the teacher's part, apart from the requirements of coursework and classroom,[56] we can only speculate as to what duties may have been required of those who taught the scripture and doctrine in Calvin's Geneva. Diligence of preparation and faithfulness to the Word of God go without saying. But, if we judge from Calvin's example alone, some care with respect to two other areas at least may have been part of their normal discipline.

The first of these has to do with methods of instruction. Certainly, Calvin offers nothing by way of analysis, description, or theory concerning the various teaching methods an instructor might use at any given time. Yet his familiarity with and use of a variety of such methods—including lecture, catechesis, reading, private tutoring, and meditation—suggest that he and the other pastors and teachers in Geneva appreciated the need for a variety of approaches to teaching, as well as the suitability of particular approaches for particular audiences, contexts, and purposes.

The lecture, for example, seems to have been largely reserved for sermons and the instruction of adults, while catechesis was primarily employed for the teaching of children. Candidates for ministry were often given private tutoring, together with a kind of mentoring that allowed them to participate in the pastoral work of their teacher.

At any rate, it seems apparent that at least some thinking went into the matter of teaching methods, that they should be appropriate in every case to the subject matter and the learner, so that the end of instruction—the fruitful life of Christian faith—might be realized in each learner.

A second area of responsibility for teachers has to do with learning objectives. Again, we are clearly reading backwards from our own perspective at this point. Even among contemporary educators discussion of learning objectives remains a somewhat contentious area. Concerning Calvin's philosophy of education, nothing concrete can be concluded as to whether or not particular courses of study or individual instructional sessions were constructed around specific learning outcomes. It is doubtless too much to believe that such was the case to any high degree of consciousness among the teachers and pastors of Geneva in Calvin's day.

Yet certain "goals" for learning were clearly in their minds at certain times. For example, with respect to the catechism, the goal for each learner is clearly stated: "When a child has been sufficiently instructed to pass on from the Catechism, he shall solemnly recite the sum of what is contained in it and he shall do this as a profession of his Christianity clearly articulated."[57] Here we may discern three particular learning objectives: (1) the child is to make an oral presentation; (2) that presentation is to consist of an accurate summation of the contents of the catechism; (3) that presentation is to include a profession of the child's personal faith in Christ. The first of these might be seen to be a *skill* goal, the second a *cognitive* goal, and the third an *affective* goal, to use contemporary terminology. It is not too much to expect that at least some such "learning objectives" must have been in the minds of Geneva's pastors and teachers with respect to those learners they were preparing for the ministry or civil government, as well as concerning the kind of instruction given by the consistory in cases of church discipline.

The overall goal of instruction in Geneva was a citizenry self-consciously submitted to the rule of Jesus Christ and bearing the fruit of that rule in their lives. In Calvin's Geneva, Christian education was regarded as more than an intellectual activity; it was the God-given means for the reformation of life, church, and society, and the pastors in Geneva, under Calvin's leadership, labored diligently to ensure that preaching and teaching were consistently directed toward these ends.

Lessons from Calvin's Example

From the example of Calvin's work in Christian education we may draw out some lessons for the church today. Christian education in churches today is in a crisis, but Christian educators hardly seem to recognize that this is so. We continue to multiply opportunities for instruction and to create new resources, employ new methods, and search out new topics for study. Yet the followers of Christ today are not becoming any better equipped for the inescapable work of engaging and critiquing contemporary culture, or the glorious challenge of creating viable Christian cultural alternatives. What can we learn from Calvin's example to help us in reforming our own practice? Three lessons in particular would seem to be important.

The utter necessity of educational reform

What Stanford Reid concludes from Calvin's example for contemporary Calvinists applies just as well to all believers today:

> From this modern Calvinists might well learn one important lesson. It is that if there is ever to be any great Calvinistic revival, it will come, and will continue, only if it is firmly based upon sound educational principles which enable it to wrestle with the problems of contemporary thought. Running away from issues raised in modern philosophy, sci-

ence and history will not solve the problem. Rather, the Calvinist must be prepared to take what the non-Christian world has discovered and thought, in order that he may re-interpret this knowledge *sub specie aeternitatis* and use it to glorify the Triune God.[58]

The manifest failure of contemporary Christian education efforts to bring about a consensus on culture matters, or to effect widespread social and cultural renewal, must not cause us to despair of the project. Many today express their distaste of doctrine and prefer to invest their "spiritual" time in fellowship and service projects rather than in the hard work of study and learning for the sake of the kingdom. Preachers have backed away from exposition of scripture and orthodox doctrine, pursuing an approach to communication that is more anecdotal and inclusive. One ad for a prominent evangelical seminary features a face-shot of a street kid, complete with earring and head scarf, and the caption, "The last thing he wants to hear is a sermon." Much of contemporary Christianity is being reduced to a dialogue over felt needs, a kind of spiritual group therapy that wants as many as possible to be able to find a secure place to be themselves before the Lord. Such an approach to Christian education can only result in further deterioration of the church's ability to fulfill its mission as the salt of the earth and the light of the world.

More than ever the Christian community needs to review its present work in Christian formation. We need to reexamine our understanding of what it means to learn—to be a disciple. We must explore new approaches to teaching and training that will equip the saints to live and serve according to the knowledge of God in the midst of a culture that is increasingly indifferent, if not hostile, to the claims of Jesus Christ. In spite of all our varied and fervent efforts to teach the people of God, our work in Christian education has not produced a body of believers who are fulfilling their callings as salt and light in a world of decay and darkness. And yet we must persevere, casting a critical eye on our own educational efforts, looking to scripture and our Christian past for new insights on how to proceed, and taking on bold and innovative educational challenges toward the end of individual and cultural renewal according to the teaching of God's Word.

Instruction for the whole person

We cannot expect to achieve such a lofty objective without more careful consideration of the needs of the individual, the church, and the society in which we live. We must begin to pursue the work of Christian education not merely as an exercise in information transfer or felt-needs satisfaction. Christian educators are called to the lofty task of educating the whole person, soul and body, for new life in the kingdom of God, and in the culture in which they live.

Christian education today is largely regarded as an enterprise of information transfer. Asked what they have been learning lately, most adult Christians will answer with some variation of a content response: "We've been studying the Book of Romans." "I've just finished a seminar on managing my money." "I'm working through a video series on the Psalms." Calvin defined true learning in terms of a growing relationship with God, expressed in growth in holiness and fulfillment of a life's calling to the praise of God and his glory. Christian educators shall be unable to achieve such goals unless we begin to discover better ways of reaching the hearts and lives of our learners, and not just their minds. The challenge to us from the example of John Calvin is for more careful preparation, more focused instruction, and more careful assessment of learning. Until we begin educating the whole person—soul and practices—for living out all the requirements of God's kingdom—righteousness, peace, and joy in the Spirit—in every area of life and culture, we will continue to drift toward the margins of society, our fervent educational activities notwithstanding.

At the same time, we shall not know improvement in our efforts at Christian formation until learners decide that, unless they are being transformed into the image of Jesus Christ, in the righteousness, peace, and joy of his Spirit, they are not really learning anything of substance about the life of faith. Learners must shake off complacency about growing in grace and turn away from being contented merely to have acquired some new information about the Bible or the life of faith. True learning engages and transforms the whole person, as Calvin reminds us; let learners begin to demand such of those who teach, and we shall begin to know renewal in this most important Christian endeavor.

A new vision of learning

Finally, we must give more attention to spelling out the kind of learning objectives that will create in our learners a vision of and earnest desire for renewed selves and a renewed culture. We must teach for specific instructional outcomes, challenging the people of God to repent of everything in their lives that is contrary to God's Word and to seek the fullness of Word and Spirit for seeing all things become new. We must challenge learners to new heights of personal holiness, greater humility in loving and serving others, improvements in excellence in their vocations, and a vision for church, society, and culture that takes seriously the promise of God's power being able to do far beyond all that we could ever ask or think (Eph. 3:20). The program of preaching and teaching that Calvin implemented in sixteenth-century Geneva exerted a transforming effect on that city. According to E. William Monter, Calvin's basic achievement

> had been to instruct an entire generation of Genevans, thoroughly and systematically, through his catechism and his sermons and his system of ecclesiastical discipline. . . . By the time Calvin died, there were few if any European cities so well indoctrinated and accustomed to rigorous discipline as was Geneva. Calvin had tried to enforce respect for the laws of God and man on a turbulent and newly independent city, and after considerable struggle he had succeeded.[59]

The influence of Calvin's work in Geneva quickly spread across Europe and ultimately to the New World, as generations of pastors, teachers, civil servants, and laypeople, trained in Geneva or by those whose programs of instruction had been adapted from that model, took their zeal for God and their biblical worldview into every area of life and culture in the lands in which they were born or to which they migrated. This is particularly true of the impact of Calvin's teaching on culture matters:

> If one stands in the line of Calvin, it is not necessary to view human cultural activity in contrast to a presumed sphere of divine activity. Culture may be viewed as an aspect of human activity, indeed in distinction to nature, but not independent of divine law, the divine plan, and divine calling. Human cultural activity may be viewed as a response to God's calling, even as all of life is, and may be judged as to whether it is carried out in accordance with His Creator-will. What is required is a reconstruction of the idea of culture, which views it within the context of divine revelation, the context within which it becomes meaningful.
> Human cultural activity, carried on in obedience to God's law, is an expression of His will. It is in line with the thought of Calvin to say that what flows from it has a place in God's plan as it relates to the end of this age and the coming of a new heavens and a new earth.[60]

In our next chapter we shall examine in greater detail the work of one heir of Calvin's program of education for personal and cultural renewal and see the powerful effects his legacy accomplished in the modern period.

Contemporary Exemplar: The BreakPoint Centurions

There exists today a growing awareness on the part of members of the Christian community of a need to become more informed on culture matters. Various efforts are under way to provide more pointed instruction to equip Christians for more effective and consistent engagement with contemporary culture, as well as in the forging of new culture with distinctly Christian features. The World Journalism Institute, sponsored by *World* magazine, hopes to raise up a new generation of Christian journalists who will be able to work for a more informed and culturally engaged Christian readership. Summit Ministries has long provided training for young people in biblical worldview thinking and living, as have many Christian colleges and universities. Lately, Focus on the Family has initiated its own effort, "The Truth Project," to provide more focused and intensive training in culture matters, and there is evidence that some megachurch leaders are beginning to think along these lines as well. The number of books and periodicals dealing with culture matters from a distinctly Christian perspective continues to increase year after year.

In 2003, recognizing both a growing interest on the part of church members for instruction in culture matters and biblical worldview, as well as a dearth of people in local churches qualified to equip those believers for living that worldview in an increasingly postmodern culture, Charles Colson and the team of the BreakPoint division of Prison Fellowship Ministries inaugurated a bold and innovative program to reach and equip hundreds of men and women, from every area of life, to step into this void and call the churches to greater consistency in living for Christ. The BreakPoint Centurions program is a one-year training regimen, involving a varied team of instructors, and employing a wide range of intensive and innovative approaches to learning, with the single objective of equipping men and women to lead their churches in more consistent Christian engagement in biblical worldview and culture matters.

In many ways the Centurions program recalls the efforts of Calvin in Geneva: it is innovative in its approach, employing a wide range of media and instructional contexts, including monthly telephone conference calls, personal mentoring, guided reading and study, interaction with contemporary culture (via film and reading), weekend residencies, and projects in ministry. The program is based on scripture, beginning with a curriculum extending over thirty weeks of daily study in scripture, using materials prepared to survey biblical teaching on the basic components of biblical worldview, and interfacing with the fathers of the early church in order to create continuity with the Christian past. In addition, each residency consists of seminars, workshops, and worship, taught by faculty members from all across the spectrum of orthodox Christianity, in which grounding in scripture is increasingly the focus. The program is open to men and women in all walks of life, who are accepted following a rigorous application process, and train in flights of 100 per year. A Centurions website allows participants to post results of their reading and study, interact with one another on matters of common concern, share new ideas, and ask questions of Centurion residency faculty members. The website is also an archive for BreakPoint staff and residency faculty to post articles of interest to be shared among the Centurions. Careful, comprehensive personal evaluations are conducted at the beginning and end of the program, in order to allow graduates to identify areas of most-needed growth and to reflect upon the ways the program has helped them to improve spiritually and in their preparation for ministry. As part of the training process Centurions must submit a three-year plan for ministry, outlining the ways they intend to put their training to use in the immediate future. Upon completion of the first year of training, additional monthly teleconference training opportunities are provided for those sensing a need in one area or another, a second year of daily devotional studies is available, and a regional development initiative has been launched to bring more effective oversight and assistance to Centurions in the field. The Centurions program is designed to help men and women discover ways of teaching and training in their own local churches in order to better equip the saints there for more consistent Christian engagement in culture matters. And it has led to the creation of new ministries and new approaches to equipping church members, providing new resources for local churches in the effort to help their people grow in understanding biblical worldview and living more consistently according to the tenets thereof.

While at this writing it is rather too early to pronounce the Centurions program an overwhelming success, the feedback from graduates is heartening. One graduate of the program has upgraded a ministry she began to high school students from her local church into a precollege training program on worldview and apologetics that is now being implemented in all fifty states and fourteen other countries. Another graduate has established an effective in-prison ministry, coupled with an out-placement program for inmates returning to society that involves using his own home as a halfway house. Many Centurions program graduates are teaching courses in their churches on worldview and culture matters, and report favorable responses from their students. One Centurion has sponsored a conference on biblical worldview in his home church in central Tennessee, in which ten of the visiting speakers were graduates of the Centurions program. One grandmother, a graduate of the program, has taken her worldview training into her ministry with small children, as well as into various ministries to women in her community. Another woman is developing a growing relationship with local artists, using her own art as a point of contact for dialogue about culture matters and biblical worldview. Another is bringing his training into a series of monthly dialogues with local Muslim leaders and has organized a citywide campaign to promote prayer for his city. Others are receiving invitations to teach biblical worldview at local schools, colleges, and universities; are creating a variety of media and computer studies programs; and are carrying the message of biblical worldview to inmates in local prisons. The most common problem reported by graduates of the program is that, once people begin to learn that training is available to help them wrestle with culture matters from a biblical and Christian perspective, the demands for their teaching quickly become more than they can fulfill.

The BreakPoint Centurions program is currently in its fourth year of operation, with over a hundred new Centurions in training and nearly three hundred active in culture matters in the field. The Centurions program has begun to take up the challenge of fostering dialogue and channeling creative energy toward a Christian consensus in culture matters. In many ways the program embodies the evangelical and cultural passions of its founder, Charles Colson, who looks at the Centurions program as an important part of what he hopes will be his legacy for the generations to come. Colson himself takes an active role in the training of each flight of Centurions, participating in residencies, answering questions posed over the Internet, joining in conference calls, and responding, as he is able, to opportunities to encourage Centurions in their work. His vision and example are a great encouragement to everyone in the program; we shall have more to say about learning from such individual leaders in cultural renewal as Charles Colson in the next chapter. The BreakPoint Centurions program is only one example of ways that contemporary Christian educators are seeking to break out of the mold of a failing educational project and discover new ways of equipping the saints for the work of ministry, for personal renewal, and the reformation of culture.

Questions for Study or Discussion

1. Have you participated in any training in a Christian approach to culture matters? Of what did that training consist? What did you gain from it?
2. Do you know of any other Christians who share your interest in culture matters? How might you join with them to form a study or discussion group? How might you benefit from such a group? How might such a group help to raise the awareness of culture matters among the members of your church?
3. What do you think are the greatest obstacles keeping people from committing to further study in culture matters? Suggest some ways you might try to help them overcome these obstacles. What might we expect of a program of Christian education where people were committed to learning to love God with all their heart, soul, mind, and strength, and their neighbors as themselves?
4. Talk to some of the people responsible for the educational program at your church. Are they open to any teaching about culture matters? In what kinds of settings might you hope to see such teaching occur? How might you help to make that a possibility?
5. Take a few moments and summarize what you have learned thus far in your reading of this book concerning a Christian approach to culture matters. Find someone with whom you can share these observations, and ask for his or her response. How might you help this person begin to be more interested in working toward a renewed consensus in culture matters?

4

Foundations for a
Christian Cultural Consensus

Abraham Kuyper and the Reformation of Culture

. . . all the issues that emerge out of the discussions about evangelical public theology today—theocracy, pluralism, freedom, the critical role of mediating structures and voluntary associations, cultures, poverty and welfare, the role of the state, coalitions with cobelligerent groups, particularly Roman Catholics—surfaced in Kuyper's own career, and his wrestling with them can be instructive for the present.

John Bolt

As for the saints in the land, they are the excellent ones, in whom is all my delight.

Psalm 16:3

ONE OF THE unhappy tendencies characteristic of certain contemporary attempts to renew Christian faith in the face of a changing cultural environment is that of setting aside the Christian past as irrelevant to the present and future needs of the church. While this is especially evident in the dramatic changes that have been effected in public worship in the evangelical community, it shows up

91

in many other ways as well. Among these is the tendency, on the part of certain pastors and church leaders, to search out new heroes and exemplars from among those who are the most outspoken against what they perceive to be the moribund forms of contemporary Christianity and who, at the same time, seem to be most successful in creating new models for other churches to emulate. Most commonly, these new heroes are the pastors of megachurches. Their latest books are eagerly anticipated and duly devoured. Their churches sponsor workshops and seminars and offer a wide range of training materials. Their websites boast scores of thousands of readers. They themselves are in increasing demand as speakers and advisers on how to configure a more relevant and successful church.

There is nothing inherently wrong or evil in this tendency, just as there is nothing inherently wrong or evil in contemporary worship. But when this tendency promotes a studied indifference to the great heritage of the faith and the achievements of previous generations, or, worse, leads to the severing of ties with the church's past, then church leaders can easily drift into tendencies and practices that can lead to heresy.[1] This problem of seeking out heroes and models only from among contemporary church leaders is simply one aspect of a wider disavowing of the Christian past, but it is perhaps the most dangerous of all these aspects, since it can easily degenerate into the formation of personality cults and the abandonment of doctrine and tradition for whatever has the appearance of relevance and success.

Happily, not everyone seeking renewal in the church has fallen to the allure of this tendency. Many still believe that the way out of our present morass can be found through a careful consideration of the Christian past.[2] As we have seen, there is much to learn from great saints of the past as we turn to the question of how to achieve a contemporary Christian consensus on culture matters. Church history, viewed in the light of scripture, holds many lessons for us as we take up the tasks of judging culture, forging new culture, and equipping ourselves for cultural engagement and renewal.

The same is true when we begin to seek out heroes or exemplars to guide us in ecclesiastical and cultural renewal. There are many great saints from the past who, in their lives and careers, exemplified the struggle to make a distinctly Christian contribution to culture matters in their own generation. St. Basil, in the fourth century, the various monastic houses of the middle ages, the early Catholic pioneers in higher education, Thomas Chalmers and William Wilberforce in the nineteenth century, Martin Luther King Jr. in the twentieth century, and many others stand out as models to whom we may turn for help in understanding how to achieve consensus and create new paths in culture matters.[3] We may richly benefit from a closer examination of how they, in their time, confronted the challenge of cultural change and led the body of Christ in seeking renewal in culture matters.

Many candidates might be referenced in an effort to identify models from church history whose lives could guide us today in seeking authentic Christian consensus on culture matters. Few Christian leaders, however, demonstrate as much in the way of cultural experience or achievement as Abraham Kuyper, the nineteenth-century Dutch theologian/journalist/politician/educator.[4] His *Lectures on Calvinism*, delivered at Princeton Theological Seminary in 1898, and still in print today, raises a standard for a Christian approach to culture from which many have benefited. In addition to this, the record of his life and insights from his many writings and speeches can help us get our bearings in the roiling seas and amid the dark clouds of cultural change that characterize our own day. Like Augustine, Kuyper maintained a lively and effective critique of the culture of his day. He also, like our Celtic Christian forebears, brought new cultural entities into being to help in furthering the work of Christ's kingdom. And, like Calvin, he invested his life in the work of education, at all levels, in order to raise up a generation of believers capable of carrying on the work of the kingdom through Christ-honoring involvement in culture matters.

This chapter will address some of the key issues relating to the involvement of Christians in culture matters by examining the career and views of Abraham Kuyper. After a brief introduction to the nineteenth century and to Kuyper himself, we will proceed to an overview of his cultural activities and views, before concluding with some observations from his example for Christians today. Kuyper provides a most useful example of the truth that culture matters, encouraging us to believe that we, as believers in changing times, may achieve a renewed consensus on this important subject. After we have considered Kuyper and the lessons from his example, we will turn to a brief discussion with one contemporary Christian cultural leader, Charles Colson, to consider how believers today might benefit from his example and that of others in seeking greater consensus on culture matters.

The Nineteenth-Century Background

The nineteenth century was a time of great intellectual, social, and cultural foment in Europe. The spirit of Enlightenment rationalism was breaking out throughout Europe in revolutionary developments in politics, science, and the arts. It was not a spirit friendly to the historic concerns of the Christian Church. Kuyper spoke and wrote often on what he referred to as "the anti-Christian character" of the century. The fruit of Enlightenment humanism was beginning to be born in the philosophical, theological, political, and cultural arenas in Kuyper's day, while, at the same time, Christianity was declining as a factor in many people's thinking and lives.

Politically, revolution—at least the fear of it—against the established social and political order was everywhere in the air. The French Revolution had sent shock waves throughout Europe that were still resonating well into the nineteenth century, leading governments to seek ways of shoring up and increasing their own power. Liberal representative governments were seeking ways of expanding the role of government in the lives of the citizenry, while, at the same time, accomplishing a shift in civil power from the old ruling classes to the elected representatives of the people. Radical political philosophies—especially Marxism—were in the air, challenging the established order and calling for social and political upheaval. Rationalist philosophers exalted the potential of human wisdom above the unchanging truths of scripture, and subjectivist theologians turned the focus of religion away from the knowledge of God to the knowledge of self. Romantic artists in all genres celebrated the experience of emotional liberation and individual freedom. Darwin and Marx reduced history to mechanics and humankind to biology and, together with new technologies and advances in all the fields of science, held out the prospect of progress on a grand scale for the human community. The new cultural revolutionaries—Goethe, Beethoven, Garibaldi, Marx, and, later, Nietzsche, Kierkegaard, and Freud—heralded an end to former ways and challenged Europeans to break away from the herd and press on toward a new humanity and a new social order.

This revolutionary thinking found its way into theology as it was taught and practiced in the Netherlands in the nineteenth century. While theologians holding to historic reformed views still held forth, their position in the church in the Netherlands was being steadily eroded by Christian humanists, ethical theologians (religious subjectivists), and outright modernists.[5] Abraham Kuyper, raised in a traditional Calvinist home, embraced more liberal views during his period of training and carried those views with him into his first pastorate. Only after his conversion to historic orthodox Christian faith during his ministry in Beesd in the 1860s did he begin to understand the revolutionary nature of his times and to think about the great and pressing issues of the day. It was during this period that he became acquainted with the antirevolutionary sentiments and convictions of such powerful figures as Guillaume Groen van Prinsterer and began to develop his own thoughts and positions concerning the application of biblical truths to the pressing concerns of culture and society.

Kuyper entered the cultural fray with a vengeance upon becoming pastor of the great church in Amsterdam. Here his strong convictions led him to become active in journalism, politics, and education on behalf of the kingdom of God. The rest of his life was devoted to speaking, writing, and working through government and the private sector on behalf of a culture and way of life that consistently reflected the wisdom and truth of God in scripture.

Cultural Achievements

Kuyper's activities in the Dutch culture of his day are well known and have been fully presented elsewhere.[6] Here we may only summarize his achievements in order to establish a platform from which to examine more carefully his views on the role of culture in the Christian life. Kuyper pursued culture matters in a wide range of disciplines and arenas. As a scholar, pastor, journalist, politician, educator, and a man of letters, he provides a rich example of Christian cultural engagement for our consideration.

Scholar

Kuyper's first involvement in the culture of his day was as a *scholar*. It was as a scholar that he first came to the attention of his contemporaries. His treatise on the reformer John a Lasco earned him widespread recognition and his doctoral degree in 1860. Kuyper would keep his hand in the work of scholarship throughout the rest of his life, ultimately producing such respected tomes as *Sacred Theology, The Work of the Holy Spirit*, and *Lectures on Calvinism*. Kuyper's lectures, essays, speeches, and longer articles reflect an ongoing awareness of scholarly developments in his day. His study and reading ranged widely—history, the arts, science, politics, philosophy, and international developments are merely a few of the areas of scholarly study that informed Kuyper's speeches, writings, and work. Kuyper did not write or speak for scholars, however. His concern was ever to reach the people of the Netherlands, to make them aware of how Enlightenment thought was eroding their Christian convictions and threatening their homes and country, and to rally them to action on behalf of a biblical worldview.

Pastor

His scholarly preparations fitted him, secondly, for *service in the church*. Kuyper entered the pastorate in 1863. During his pastoral career he served churches in Beesd, Utrecht, and Amsterdam, and gained a reputation as a persuasive preacher. Kuyper remained a pastor until his entry into politics in 1874. Thereafter, he continued to serve the church as a ruling elder. His work as a pastor helped to create an important bridge for Kuyper's later work between the life of the mind and the spirit and the everyday lives of people, in their homes, neighborhoods, and occupations. His interaction with church members alerted him to the powerful effects of ideas on daily life. As people were wooed away from trust in the scriptures and faith in the sovereign God, and fell under the thrall of religious subjectivism and Enlightenment rationalism, they experienced a loss of hope and purpose, and felt their lives slipping into irrelevance and moral compromise. Kuyper used his work as a pastor to expose the dark undercurrents of contemporary thought and to call the people of God to faith in his Word. Beginning in 1867 and extending throughout the 1890s, Kuyper played a leading role in efforts to reform the church in Holland, culminating in his ouster from the now-liberal state church and the creation of the new denomination, the Reformed Churches in the Netherlands, in 1892.

Journalist

Kuyper's involvement with the institutions of Dutch culture continued to expand when, in the 1860s, he began to write devotional and theological material for the weekly journal *The Herald*, of which he became editor in 1871. In 1872 he founded and edited the daily political journal *The Standard*. Thus, in the third place, he was now fully engaged in the world of Dutch *journalism*, in addition to his roles in church and home. His daily and weekly writings achieved a wide readership and served as the forge in which his political and cultural thinking were refined, as well as the reservoir from which many of his larger and more lasting works were drawn.

Politician

Fourth, at about this time Kuyper began to take an active role in Dutch *politics* and was elected a member of parliament in 1874. In this setting he was thrust into leadership of the Anti-Revolutionary Party, the newly organized political movement determined to resist the revolutionary spirit of the age, preserve the traditional culture of the Netherlands, and advance a Christian social and moral agenda throughout the nation. Kuyper led his party in seeking social reform in a wide range of areas, among them, labor and educational reform. In his work as a politician he demonstrated brilliance in forging political alliances among Christians from various communions, including Roman Catholics. He believed that matters of great public moment required true Christians to set aside their differences and, rallying together around their love for Christ and the authority of his Word, unite in political struggle to advance a kingdom agenda. For his brilliance and proven leadership in these efforts, Kuyper was elected prime minister of the Netherlands, in which office he served his country from 1901 to1905.

Education

Education in general, and higher education in particular, became, in the fifth place, passionate interests for Kuyper from 1860 on. He led the movement for free schools in the Netherlands, schools not subject to government control and thus able to preserve and advance the interests of Christian parents. He was instrumental in founding the Free University of Amsterdam in 1880—again, "free" in the sense of being separate from state control. There he also served as instructor and rector.

Man of letters

Finally, throughout his career, Kuyper excelled as *a man of letters*. He wrote devotional material, scholarly books, cultural and political criticism, and speeches and sermons on a wide range of subjects. In his writing and speeches we may discover the four key cultural ideas that pervade his life and work: *antithesis, sphere sovereignty,* the absolute *lordship of Christ,* and *freedom of the conscience.* We must examine each of these briefly.

Kuyper's Cultural Ideas

Antithesis

Kuyper, like Augustine, came to see that a great struggle was being fought on all fronts between truth and error, light and darkness, the kingdom of God and the kingdoms of men, which he regarded as enemies to the gospel. His broad involvement in cultural matters was impelled by his sense of the need to strike a blow for truth wherever its enemies seemed particularly active or vulnerable at any moment, or where the forces of truth needed shoring up. Of this antithesis Kuyper wrote in 1898,

> There is no doubt then that Christianity is imperilled by great and serious dangers. Two *life systems* are wrestling with one another, in mortal combat. Modernism is bound to build a world of its own from the data of natural man, and to construct man himself from the data of nature; while, on the other hand, all those who reverently bend the knee to Christ and worship Him as the Son of the living God, and God Himself, are bent upon saving the "Christian Heritage." This *is the* struggle in Europe, this is *the* struggle in America, and this also, is the struggle for principles in which my own country is engaged, and in which I myself have been spending all my energy for nearly forty years.[7]

Kuyper recognized early on that the danger of the modernist impulse was its desire to effect uniformity in life, to achieve a great "leveling" of society, a sameness and blandness that subjects all to lockstep conformity to ideals promulgated by an intellectual and political elite. He believed that this tendency ran contrary to the teaching of scripture and the ordinances of God, and called the people of the Netherlands to struggle against the modern spirit with all their strength.[8] As Kuyper saw it, this great struggle—this antithesis—had to be waged on every front where issues of truth could be fruitfully engaged, and by means of every available resource, tool, and institution. The opponents of truth were attempting to storm the redoubts of culture in the arenas of politics, science, education, the arts, and even the church. Kuyper believed that the Christian community needed to prepare for a concerted effort to resist these assaults and reclaim the whole vast field of culture for Christ. To this end, as we have noted, he often supported and took the lead in joint undertakings with a wide range of Christian communities. Kuyper called the Christians of the Netherlands to begin with themselves and to create an alternative culture that could stand up against and prevail over the revolutionary cultural proposals and paradigms gaining currency across Europe:

> With a view to our own struggle, I mean that those who still have faith and discern the danger of blurring the boundaries must start by drawing a line around *their own circle,* must develop *a life of their own* within that circle, must *render account* for the life thus constituted, and so acquire the maturity needed for the struggle they must at some point accept.[9]

If the Christian community could accept the call to consensus and collaboration in culture matters, Kuyper believed, "there *would* be resistance, a spontaneously working force that blessed the entire nation and made itself felt in church, state, and society by virtue of the reality of your conduct and the fact of your existence."[10] A reformed community of the followers of Christ would reform everything in which they were involved, and the antithetical struggle of the day would issue in kingdom blessings for the entire nation.

Sphere sovereignty

Kuyper believed that all the social and cultural spheres of human life were meant to function according to divine purpose, each by its own unique set of principles in the light of God's Word. The great struggle of his day was to shore up those areas of Dutch life where the "Christian heritage" was under assault and sagging, and to open new fronts into areas where the light of the gospel had ceased to shine or had not yet begun to reform human life. In his inaugural address for the Free University of Amsterdam, Kuyper set forth his view of sphere sovereignty:

> There is a domain of nature in which the Sovereign exerts power over matter according to fixed laws. There is also a domain of the personal, of the household, of science, of social and ecclesiastical life, each of

which obeys its own laws of life, each subject to its own chief. A realm of thought where only the laws of logic may rule. A realm of conscience where none but the Holy One may give sovereign commands. Finally, a realm of faith where the person alone is sovereign who through that faith consecrates himself in the depths of his being.[11]

Kuyper believed that the interaction of these various spheres, as they discovered and followed their divinely appointed courses, could make for a harmonious and prosperous society:

> The cogwheels of all these spheres engage each other, and precisely through that interaction emerges the rich, multifaceted multiformity of human life. Hence also arises the danger that one sphere in life may encroach on its neighbor like a sticky wheel that shears off one cog after another until the whole operation is disrupted. Hence also the raison d'être for the special sphere of authority that emerged in the State. It must provide for sound mutual interaction among the various spheres, insofar as they are externally manifest, and keep them within just limits.[12]

Kuyper's commitment to the concept of sphere sovereignty was worked out not only in theoretical terms, but practical ones as well, as he carried his views into the various arenas of culture and attempted to define and operate on the principles he regarded as germane to each of the spheres of home, church, politics, journalism, science, and education. His ability to weave his views and convictions into each area without compromising the unique limits and duties of each sphere (think of his insistence on his new university being "free") indicates something of his ability to make sphere sovereignty an actual working principle of a Christian approach to culture.

Kuyper believed that everything in life reflected the divine thinking of God and was uniquely designed and constituted to work toward the end of glorifying him. Every creature and every institution thus had its own integrity, according to the divine Logos and Decree. As men, together, submitted their minds to the revelation of God in scripture, they could discover and bring that uniqueness to full and glorious expression in obedience to the Word.[13]

The absolute lordship of Christ

Kuyper taught that every sphere of life in the great antithesis existed under the lordship of King Jesus. Ultimately each and all must be made to serve him. Kuyper did not accept the sacred/secular dichotomy that characterizes certain aspects of social life today, and of various contemporary Christian approaches to culture. He wrote,

Man in his antithesis as fallen *sinner* or self-developing *natural creature* returns again as the "subject that thinks" or "the object that prompts thought" in every department, in every discipline, and with every investigator. Oh, no single piece of our mental world is to be hermetically sealed off from the rest, and there is not a square inch in the whole domain of our human existence over which Christ, who is Sovereign over *all,* does not cry: "Mine!"[14]

Kuyper devoted his considerable energies throughout his life to the task of reconciling as much of his world as he could to Jesus Christ. Working in numerous cultural arenas, and through a wide range of cultural vehicles, he managed to express his belief in the lordship of Christ cogently and with effect.

One of the important implications of this view was that, in any aspect of human life, the spiritual realm must have priority over the temporal. Kuyper wrote, "Whoever neglects to maintain the autonomy of the spiritual over against the material in his point of departure will eventually come to the idolization of matter by way of the adoration of man."[15] This explains why so much of Kuyper's labor over the years was spent in devotional writing, and in insisting on the importance of such spiritual disciplines as fasting in the life of the believer.[16] He believed that no one would have the intellectual and physical stamina, or the wisdom and determination of will, to carry on the struggle of the great antithesis in the realm of culture if he did not first and continuously yield his soul to the lordship of Christ through the practices of worship and piety. He taught that only those who knew the inner illumination of the Holy Spirit, shaping and reforming their lives from the inside out, would be able to follow him in the reformation of culture.[17] Unless Christ is Lord first of all in our hearts, we will not serve him as Lord in our culture.

Freedom of conscience

In this great work of reconciliation—the struggle for a proper sovereignty of the spheres of life, which is the struggle of the great antithesis—humankind's only tools in winning its enemies to its views are reason and persuasion. Kuyper did not believe in coercing people to

live contrary to their own convictions, that is, as long as social life was
not imperiled. He worked for a true pluralism of worldviews—what
Richard John Neuhaus would call an "open public square"—where
none was given legal favor over the others, but all could argue their
virtues openly, leaving the outcome to sound judgment. Kuyper believed in "the sovereignty of conscience as the palladium of all personal liberty, in this sense—that conscience is never subject to man
but always and ever to God Almighty."[18] Consequently,

> we must employ *persuasion* to the exclusion of *coercion* in all spiri-
> tual matters. Someday there will be coercion, when Christ descends
> in majesty from the heavens, breaks the anti-Christian powers with a
> rod of iron, and, in the words of Psalm 2, dashes them in pieces like
> a potter's vessel [v. 9]. He has a right to this because he knows the
> hearts of all and will be the judge of all. But we do not. To us it is
> given to fight with spiritual weapons and to bear our cross in joyful
> discipleship.[19]

Kuyper's commitment to persuasion helps us to understand why
writing and public speaking were such important parts of his work to
achieve cultural consensus in the Netherlands. Kuyper was a master
speaker, a careful writer, and a persuasive arguer in all his words. He
encourages us to believe that, even against the growing darkness of
our own cultural times, a commitment to persuasion, resting firmly
on the lordship of Christ and the work of the Holy Spirit, might yet
be a powerful tool for achieving consensus and reform on culture
matters.

These four convictions—the idea of antithesis, the notion of sphere
sovereignty, belief in the absolute lordship of Christ, and commitment to freedom of conscience—come up over and over in Kuyper's
writings. They characterize as well all his life's work. They mark
out the broad parameters of his philosophy of culture and serve to
make his involvement in the culture of his day particularly powerful
and lasting.

Culture Matters: Lessons and Applications

The primary lesson for Christians today that emerges from the
example of Abraham Kuyper's involvement in the culture of his day
is that culture matters, and, because it matters, Christians should

work together to articulate and practice an approach to culture that is consistent with their heritage and views. Culture cannot be ignored, and it must not be regarded lightly. It has the potential to make an important contribution to the work of God's kingdom and the progress of his truth, as Kuyper's example shows. Kuyper's example suggests four lessons about the importance of culture matters and encourages us to three applications for renewing consensus in culture matters in our day.

Culture matters to God

First, culture matters because God rules over it. Concerning Calvinism, Kuyper wrote,

> In this also, placing itself before the face of God, it has not only honored *man* for the sake of his likeness to the Divine image, but also *the world* as a Divine creation, and has at once placed to the front the great principle that there is a *particular grace* which works Salvation, and also *a common grace* by which God, maintaining the life of the world, relaxes the curse which rests upon it, arrests its process of corruption, and thus allows the untrammelled development of our life in which to glorify Himself as Creator.[20]

As part of the divine creation, and, in particular, of the way human beings, the image-bearers of God, express themselves in the world, culture falls under the scope of God's sovereignty and the principle of his common grace, and should serve the purposes of his glory. Thus, we may not treat culture with *indifference*, because God does not. Neither may we simply *ignore or avoid* it, for it is central to our existence in the world. And we must not *accommodate* to whatever cultural expressions come along, as some of these shall surely be found to be contrary to divine purposes. Instead, Christians must work for a culture that expresses their unique self-consciousness as the redeemed of the Lord, and their mission of reconciling all things in the world back to their Creator. But that culture must be neither trivial nor narrow; rather, it must reach out in the grace and truth of God to embrace all that falls under the divine lordship.

At the same time, we must remember that, while culture is a primary way that we as believers express our existence *coram deo*, before the face of God, it is not the primary means whereby the truth of God and God's kingdom rule make progress on the earth. That is the particular task of preaching (which itself, however, can be regarded as a cultural activity: cf. 1 Cor. 9:19–23; Acts 14 and 17). Culture serves as a backdrop against which the work of preaching and making disciples can go forward with greatest benefit. The more that backdrop reflects the divine Logos and Decree, the greater will be the blessings of God for citizens and nation alike. At the same time, culture serves the followers of Christ as a way to express their loyalty to him as Lord. It is how they bring to light the beauty and truth with which they are infused by virtue of being, together, the image-bearers of God,[21] and contribute to weaving the social and cultural backdrop that honors God and blesses the nation. Culture matters are important because they can reflect the purpose, plan, and character of God; however, culture is not the primary means of advancing the gospel, and it should not be intended or employed as such.

Kuyper shows us that culture must matter to us because it matters so much to God, whom we serve. God's rule over all of life includes all culture as well. As the vicegerents of God (cf. Gen. 1:26–28; Ps. 8), Christians must pay careful attention to the culture that confronts them, the culture they create, and the culture they embrace as they carry out their kingdom mission in the world, always seeking forms and expressions of culture that honor God as Creator and Lord and support and further his purposes among humankind.

Sin corrupts culture

Second, culture matters because it is so often turned to sinful purposes, purposes that oppose the progress of the gospel and would rob God of his glory. Kuyper summarized this tendency as he observed it in his own day:

> In place of the worship of the most high God came, courtesy of Humanism, the worship of *man*. Human destiny was shifted from *heaven* to *earth*. The Scriptures were unraveled and the Word of God shamefully repudiated in order to pay homage to the majesty of *Reason*. The institution of the church was twisted into an instrument for undermining the faith and later for destroying it. The public school had to wean the rising generation away from the piety of our fathers. Universities have been refashioned into institutions at which Darwinism violates the spiritual nobility of humanity by denying its creation in the image of God. Hedonism replaced heaven-mindedness. And *emancipation* became the watchword by which people tampered with the bond of marriage, with the respect children owe their parents, with the moral

seriousness of our national manners. This went on until first Philosophy, then Socialism raised its voice. The former replaced *certainty* in our hearts with *doubt;* the latter, logically developing upper-class liberal theory, applied to the *money* and *goods* of the owners what the liberal already had the audacity to do against God and his anointed King.[22]

Sin tempts us to separate culture matters from God. To paraphrase Kuyper's comments about science, sin leads us to disconnect our cultural activities from God, to steal them from God, and, finally, to turn them against him.[23] Hence, again, we cannot expect to do effective battle in the arenas of culture unless we are first and at all times doing battle in the struggle for our souls.

The institutions, artifacts, and conventions that make up any culture are not neutral instruments designed only to enhance survival or the enjoyment of life. They are part and parcel of a worldview that, in the antithesis between the kingdoms of light and darkness, cannot possibly occupy some middle ground. Either culture will be consciously developed and employed for the advancement of the kingdom of God, or it will fall into the hands of those who seek nothing more than the fuller realization of the next human agenda or scheme. *Indifference* to culture therefore is tantamount to abandoning the high ground to the adversary. *Avoidance* of it is impossible. *Narrow selectivity* in the creation of a distinctively Christian culture leaves the most powerful aspects of culture in the hands of God's enemies. Cultural *accommodation* to contemporary cultural forms can be tantamount to community betrayal. A self-consciously biblical approach to culture is required, one that looks to God, speaking in the Word of God, to guide us in thinking about how best to put culture to use for our benefit and his glory. But such an approach to culture cannot stand alone; it must support and give way to the preaching of the kingdom of God as the centerpiece of the church's mission and must not lose sight of the fact that the kingdom of God, while intimately associated with culture, is greater than culture, as we shall see.

Called to culture

Third, culture matters because it is central to the calling of the redeemed of the Lord. Ours is no *merely* spiritual calling; rather, it is a spiritual calling intended to affect every area of human life and interest. Kuyper wrote that in a fallen, sinful world, people are called "to

struggle valiantly against the powers that would destroy [them]. . . .
God commands [them] to work, to labor, to struggle with nature."[24]
He was committed to the belief that "the duty is now emphasized of
serving God *in*the world, in every position of life."[25] Every Christian
is called to engage in the great work of subduing the earth and all the
culture in it, so that God may be glorified in the works of our hands
as though they were God's own:

> Live within the will of God, doing your work according to His will—not
> because the law demands it, nor to earn your daily bread as if your
> livelihood depended upon it; but for God's sake, always motivated by
> the desire to honor Him. Let your life be one of continuous service of
> love, a service which never grows irksome, a service which will hallow
> even the smallest task. Seek not the external, the visible, that which
> the world chooses as its goal. But that which is invisible, the hidden
> power behind the things which we see—in short, seek the Kingdom
> of God, where God is enthroned and self is denied; seek all that is
> right, all that is in conformity with His righteousness; seek these things
> not only in seasons of prayer and meditation and worship, but always,
> in every situation, in every daily task.[26]

We have already seen that involvement in culture is unavoidable,
and necessary. The only question is *how* we shall be involved. The
redeemed of the Lord are called to culture, and, as in every other
area of their lives, they must learn to serve the lordship of Jesus and
the cause of his kingdom in culture matters.

The power of culture

Finally, Kuyper shows us that culture matters because culture has
great power. Redeemed culture—culture used under the lordship of
Christ—is most conducive to promoting the well-being of people
and the glory of God, while sinful culture undermines human dignity
and leads to social and moral degeneration. Kuyper wrote of the
potential of various aspects of culture to accomplish the purposes of
benefiting men and glorifying God. Of science he wrote that it had
the potential to

> attain unto that high, dominant and prophetical character by which
> it not only liberates itself from the cosmos, but also understands it,
> enables its devotees to take active part in it, and partially forsee [*sic*]
> its future development.

Hence, it is not enough that the knowledge of God, which, as a flower in the bud, is hidden and covered in the Scripture, is set forth by us in its excellency; but that bud must be unfolded, the flower must make exhibition of its beauty, and scent the air with its fragrance. This can be done spiritually by piety of mind, practically by deeds of faith, aesthetically in hymns, parenetically in exhortation, but must also be done by scientific exposition and description.[27]

Kuyper also believed that the arts held great potential for bringing honor and glory to God and much blessing to people. He regarded art "as one of the richest gifts of God to mankind."[28] He particularly appreciated the art of the Dutch baroque period, which showed the beauty and love of God in the simplest and meanest of subjects.[29]

His high regard for such aspects of culture as scholarly endeavor, journalism, government and politics, and education is revealed in his own career. What he wrote of government could be equally applied to all these, and to all other aspects of culture as well:

Therefore, in the affairs of the nation, as well as in all other spheres of life, the Christian is called upon to fight the fight of faith, to be a soldier of Jesus Christ. . . . So then everyone who believes in Christ as the sovereign Ruler over our country *must,* if he has true patriotic love, rise to the defense of the honor of Christ in our politics. So long as we do this with all resolution, wisdom, and our combined strength, the possibility still remains that the spirit of apostasy can be arrested. . . . The magistrate is an instrument of "common grace," to thwart all license and outrage and to shield the good against the evil. But he is more. Besides all this he is instituted by God as *His Servant,* in order that he may preserve the glorious work of God, in the creation of humanity, from total destruction.[30]

Given the great power of culture to serve God and bless humankind, all Christians, whatever their approach to culture, must be willing to begin seeking together a more comprehensive, consistent, practical, and consensual philosophy of culture matters than currently exists within our community.

In addition to these four lessons we can identify three applications from Kuyper's example, three steps that Christians can begin to take that can help them to experience a fuller and more powerful approach to culture together, and to articulate a more consistent and cogent Christian approach to culture matters than presently exists.

Take up the challenge of culture

First, as a community, we must accept both the inevitability and the potentiality of culture. We can neither escape nor avoid culture; it is essential to our existence as human beings. At the same time, we must neither take culture for granted nor isolate the distinctively Christian element of our culture to some narrowly defined focus. Kuyper warned against allowing our cultural thinking and activities to be limited to the sphere of the church.[31] Culture is as broad as life, encompassing all the artifacts, institutions, and conventions that make up our experience in the world, and by which we both define ourselves and sustain and enrich our lives. Culture defines our lives at home, on the job, in our communities, churches, voluntary associations, and avocations. It includes the language through which we communicate, the work ethic that characterizes us on the job or in school, and our political convictions, as well as our daily routines, tastes in fashion, manners, and even the decor of our homes and our personal habits. Culture is expressed by our preferences in music, entertainment, and personal enrichment. We are immersed in culture and cultural activities all our waking moments. We cannot avoid culture, and we must strive to make certain that, whatever cultural activity we are involved in at any given moment, we are doing it unto the glory of God (1 Cor. 10:31).

Thus, Christians must work together to articulate a more thoroughly Christian and more consistently practical approach to culture than we have heretofore worked out. Our experience in this generation reveals little to set us off as a people distinguished in all the areas listed above as holding to a unique view of our lives in the world. Christians must begin to expect of their leaders—pastors, educators, church officers, and Bible teachers, as well as theologians and philosophers—more consistent and concrete instruction in a more consistently Christian approach to culture, equipping them for the challenge of taking up culture as part of their pursuit of the kingdom of God and his righteousness. For those uninstructed in such thinking, Kuyper's *Lectures on Calvinism* would be a good place to start (it was for Chuck Colson, as we shall see). Here readers can begin to train their minds in how to think about culture matters from a more consistently Christian perspective. Certainly we will not agree with all that we find there, and much of it will be seen to be out of date. However, the principles articulated in Kuyper's seminal work can at least provide a platform for beginning to think more consistently together concerning culture matters from a Christian point of view, and for beginning to nurture a vision of more consistent and comprehensive involvement in culture matters by the members of the Christian community. From there, additional studies in other works on Christian culture, but especially in the Bible itself, will prove rewarding. As church leaders grow in their understanding of a biblical approach to culture, their sermons, lessons, and writings will begin to help the other members of their communities to understand what is required of and promised to them in this important undertaking. Together we may begin to learn that our daily interactions and involvement with culture can be a means of demonstrating a more consistent witness to God and his kingdom.

Pay attention to contemporary culture

Second, we must, as a community, begin to pay more attention to the times in which we live and to the state of the great antithesis as it exists in our day. What Kuyper observed about the spiritual polarization of his time is, if anything, even more pronounced today. Only as we are careful to assess the state of culture around us will we be able to see where the lines of battle are being drawn and to engage the adversaries of God's kingdom more fruitfully. Like the sons of Issachar, we must work hard to understand the times in which we live, so that we might be better able to know what we should do in culture matters and everything else (1 Chron. 12:32).

This may prove to be the greatest challenge for members of the Christian community, for it will certainly require of us more and more that we "come out from among them . . . and touch not the unclean thing" (2 Cor. 6:17, KJV). We cannot expect to embrace a more consistent Christian pattern of cultural involvement if our lives in culture are entirely taken up with the views and practices of the world. Yet we shall not be able to determine the areas where we are, in effect, cooperating with the enemy until we begin the hard work of critiquing the culture around us, and then of evaluating, from a Christian perspective, what we are reading, watching, or listening to; the extent to which our work, manners, and habits reflect worldly rather than eternal convictions; or the true nature of our aspirations, commitments, and entertainments. As we begin to examine together the culture of the world in the light of our growing Christian understanding of culture, we will be better able to determine those areas in which our own thinking and practice must begin to change.

This means that we cannot entirely separate ourselves from the culture of the world, or from those for whom that culture is home. Christian leaders must study to understand the times in which we live and to interpret those times for the people they are called to serve. All members of the community must have at least enough understanding of the culture of our day to be able to avoid being tossed about and carried about by every wind of doctrine or taken captive by vain philosophies (Eph. 4:14; Col. 2:8). And we must use our understanding of the times to help us in determining how to construct a culture that is distinctly kingdom-like in its expression, how to educate and equip ourselves and our children for taking up the challenge of culture matters, and how best to reach for Christ those who are yet captive in the culture of our day.

Pursue culture for the glory of God

Finally, we must resolve to use our involvement in culture solely for the glory of God and the progress of his kingdom. We can no longer afford the luxury of mere self-indulgence as a motive for cultural activity, whether that indulgence takes the form of indifference, avoidance, narrowness, accommodation, overburdening, or transformation. Christians must discover ways of working toward a new consensus on culture matters, one that includes at least some elements that all participants can embrace. We must learn to dialogue and discuss culture matters with one another, and develop our powers of persuasion as we take the challenge of culture matters into broader arenas. As we have seen, the stakes involved in the Christian community's continuing to be divided over matters of culture are simply too high. We must join together in the struggle for a renewed Christian consensus on culture matters. In particular, I would make three observations concerning our involvement in culture as it relates to our lives in the kingdom of God.

First, culture is critical in expressing our kingdom citizenship. If all that we do is consciously designed to reflect the glory of God, and if we are consistently seeking the kingdom and his righteousness as our first priority in all things (Matt. 6:33), then our cultural activities, preferences, and practices will necessarily reveal us to be a people different from those around us in the world. The nature of the kingdom of God—its righteousness, justice, peace, and joy (Rom. 14:17)—will begin to come through more clearly and consistently in all our involvement with culture. Sometimes this may not be as pronounced and obvious as at other times; however, at all times a greater consistency of kingdom-consciousness in our cultural activities will contribute to our being more readily identifiable as a people for God's own possession, as we, in all aspects of our lives, declare by our culture the many excellencies of the One who has called us out of darkness into his glorious light (1 Peter 2:10). As Kuyper and the Christian community of his day demonstrated, by concentrating on our own critique of contemporary culture, and working together to create new cultural forms, and to become better equipped for engagement in culture matters, we in our day may also expect the Lord to bless our efforts in this vein as we devote them and ourselves together to the pursuit of his kingdom as of first priority.

Second, such kingdom-consciousness in our cultural activities cannot help but advance the kingdom of God in this world. This will happen in two ways. First, in our own lives we can expect to see greater evidence of the rule of God's righteousness, peace, and joy as we lay aside the works of darkness and take up our new life in Christ in a more consistent and comprehensive manner. Second, as people are exposed to our good works through various interactions with our kingdom culture, we should expect many of them to note the differences evident in our way of life—the purpose and hope by which we live—and to inquire as to the reason of the hope that they see in us (1 Peter 3:15). As our renewed cultural lives open up doors of opportunity for us to explain our kingdom calling and motivation, we may even be able, as the Spirit enables, to persuade some of our contemporaries to join us in this life of glorifying God and enjoying him forever (Matt. 5:16). Thus, the kingdom of God, the rule of righteousness, justice, and peace, will continue to increase on earth until he comes (Isa. 9:7).

Third, however, we must not make the mistake of thinking that in our cultural activities we can exhaust the kingdom of God. The kingdom of God is greater and more expansive than culture. This is so because, in the first place, as Kuyper reminds us, it is an internal kingdom, accomplishing its transformational rule first of all in the hearts, minds, and consciences of men and women. The affections and understandings that people bring to bear on their cultural and other tasks are the fruit of the work of God ruling in their hearts. These cannot be manufactured as one makes culture; rather, they are prior to culture and essential for it, and depend on the faithful preaching of the Word of Christ, the disciplines of Christian piety, and abiding in the Word. As we seek the kingdom of God through the practices of spiritual transformation, God works within us to will and do of his good pleasure, shaping our hearts and minds so that they, in turn, can fit us for lives of kingdom obedience (Phil. 2:12–13). Thus, the work of God's kingdom within us equips us for the work of expressing and advancing his kingdom through our cultural activities in the world.

In the second place, our cultural involvement does not exhaust the kingdom of God, for that kingdom will not come to its full fruition until King Jesus returns to take his kingdom citizens unto himself, to vanquish his remaining enemies, to make a new heaven and a new earth, and to establish his glorious reign with his saints forever. In this respect our cultural activities can only foreshadow the kingdom in its final state, and give us a foretaste of it; yet, in so doing, they strengthen our blessed hope, excite us concerning the full inheritance that awaits us, and inspire us to ever greater achievements for the glory of God and God's kingdom.

Contemporary Exemplar: Charles Colson

As Christians we must not neglect culture matters in our work of making all the nations disciples; instead, let us begin to explore ways of working together for a more effective cultural consensus. Our present state of division concerning culture requires that we begin to seek a more consistent, more powerful, and more consensual approach to culture than is currently in evidence. As we undertake this important task, Abraham Kuyper can serve as a guide and an example of cultural involvement from whom we can benefit. From his life and work we learn that culture matters; thus, the more care and attention we pay to culture matters, and the greater our diligence and consistency in applying what we learn, the more we can expect that our approach to culture will bring honor to God and will serve the purposes of his kingdom in this world.

In our day we are blessed with many active and effective Christian men and women whose example of leadership in areas of culture can inspire and guide us as we labor for a renewed consensus in culture matters. Joni Eareckson Tada continues to inspire many for a renewed awareness and appreciation of the disabled among us. Christian businessmen like Richard DeVos and Frederick W. Smith have pioneered approaches to business that have opened doors of opportunity for service and prosperity for many. There is no shortage of educators, artists, writers, and professionals who are seeking to embody in their cultural lives as well as their personal lives the kingdom principles by which Christ is making all things new.

One man especially stands out in our day as a kind of contemporary Kuyper. Charles Colson's work in prison reform, spiritual renewal, institution building, education, public policy, and Christian letters makes him an excellent example to turn to for guidance in culture matters. The following interview was conducted in the spring of 2006, as Mr. Colson was in the midst of a transition to new and more challenging endeavors in culture matters.

Chuck, I know that you will be somewhat reluctant to be compared to Abraham Kuyper as an example of Christian involvement in culture. But his example has inspired you in many ways, isn't that so?

Kuyper's example has certainly informed my life and work in many significant ways. In the early 1980s I was challenged by my friend Jim Kennedy to read Kuyper's *Lectures on Calvinism* given at Princeton in 1898. Though Jim actually goaded me into it, halfway through the *Lectures* I realized that they were life-changing. All at once I saw that Christianity was not just my experience with Jesus, as important as that had been to me, but it was a way of looking at all of life, seeing the world through God's eyes. It is a comprehensive system of thought, a way to know reality and ultimate truth. Shortly thereafter I came to realize that the problems in the criminal justice system that I was working in so fervently were never going to be solved by simply going into the prisons, or even fixing up some of the structural problems in the justice system. The reason for the huge upsurge in prison population during the 1980s was the breakdown of the family—a worldview issue, precisely the kind of thing Kuyper talked about. And so by the mid-80s I was giving my own Kuyperian lectures, if you will. I began writing a regular column for *Christianity Today* on a biblical perspective on current events. And soon thereafter began the BreakPoint radio program. All of this is traceable to Kuyper's influence on my life. I have continued to study him avidly. I particularly enjoyed biographies in which I have found some similarities in the way we approached public policy questions. I'm humbled any time to be compared with Kuyper, even in a small way.

You seem to have become concerned about Christian cultural involvement very early on following your conversion to Christ. To what do you attribute this? Further, I know that you have worked very hard to equip yourself with a biblical worldview, such as you articulate in How Now Shall We Live? *What have been some of the formative influences on your thinking? Who are some of the people who have helped you along in this journey?*

The reason I became concerned with Christian cultural engagement early in my ministry was the realization that one could fix the prison problems, one could even evangelize many of the inmates, and never solve the *real* problem. The reason for rising crime and burgeoning crime rates was becoming clear: it was not environment, poverty, race, or other sociological factors, as so many people thought in the early twentieth century, indeed, through the '60s. Rather, it was a moral question. Professors Samenow and Yochelson did a study called "The Criminal Personality," in 1977. They found that the cause of crime was not what sociologists had believed, or for that matter, politicians during the Great Society; but it was individuals making wrong moral choices. Samenow and Yochelson did a 17-year longitudinal study of inmates coming out of the DC system. It was very compelling evidence.

It was further confirmed by the work of Professors Wilson and Hernstein at Harvard, in 1986. They wrote *Crime and Human Nature*, in which they found that the cause of crime was the lack of moral training during the morally formative years. It became obvious to me that, if my mission field was the prisons, I had to care about the values by which Americans were ordering their lives.

It was during this same period that I did a lot of reading about William Wilberforce, the great British parliamentarian who waged a 20-year campaign to abolish the slave trade. Wilberforce had been converted to Christ through the Wesley Awakening, and he sacrificed his political career to fight the abominable practice of packing black bodies in the holds of ships and transporting them to the western hemisphere. One day, reflecting on his mission, Wilberforce wrote that "God has laid before me two great objectives; the abolition of the slave trade and the reformation of manners."

That was it! I understood, as Wilberforce had, that if we're going to make any change in American life, we not only have to attack the systems which are broken, but we have to change the habits, dispositions, manners, and attitudes of the people. In other words, political reform has to be accompanied by moral and cultural reform.

In addition to the example of Wilberforce and the teaching of Kuyper, I have been profoundly affected by Francis Schaeffer's writings. He was, in many respects, a modern-day Kuyper. I have read many other modern writers who embrace worldview thinking and have been inspired by those who challenge us to think Christianly—all the way from Harry Blamires to Neal Plantinga and Mark Noll. If you look at the bibliographies in my books, you will see the writers to whom I am most deeply indebted.

Prison Fellowship, the ministry you founded, has recently undergone a revision of its mission statement to incorporate the work of BreakPoint, Prison Fellowship's new worldview division. How do you see these two agencies working together for the progress of the kingdom?

Prison Fellowship has, for the past ten years, had a ministry not only to prisoners but for the reform of culture. We have now institutionalized that, so to speak, in a mission statement that talks about transformation of prisoners and their families along with the transformation of communities by renewing the thinking of believers. This is the same parallelism Wilberforce expressed. I'd like to think this combination can be a model for the church. The church has to fulfill both the Great Commission, that is, to make disciples, and the Cultural Commission, that is, to cultivate and till, name the animals, take dominion, be fruitful and multiply. We have to care about God's world and bringing his truth and righteousness to bear in every walk of life. When the church sees its mission as doing both of these, inevitably people will not only come to Christ but the culture surrounding us will be transformed. To see both these commissions, which I hope the church will be inspired to see, perhaps through the example of our ministry, is the key to any hope for revival or awakening in America.

You are presently investing the majority of your time in training a new generation of men and women to lead the churches in more consistent Christian involvement in culture matters—the Centurions. Are you encouraged by what you have seen thus far?

When I was preparing to sign a contract with Tyndale House for *How Now Shall We Live?* we contracted with George Barna for a study of how many Christians understood worldview and how many thought it was an important issue. His findings were discouraging. Only a tiny percentage understood what worldview is, and only 4 percent wanted more materials. But today that has changed. *How Now Shall We Live?*, written with Nancy Pearcey, has sold almost half a million copies, and is used on campuses and in study groups in churches. It's had a tremendous ministry. Today we're finding a new awakening to the importance of worldview and culture matters, and to the ways in which these can be taught. Look at the Christian magazines and you'll see ads for worldview conferences (not all of them worldview the way I would describe it). But it's an encouraging sign that there is so much interest and activity today, whereas ten years ago there was practically none. I'm finding, through teaching the Centurions, through our youth programs, and through a new curriculum that has been developed with Rick Warren,[32] that there is a growing receptiveness for material on worldview and culture matters, and a great responsiveness on the part of those we teach. We've had three classes of Centurions complete their initial training, and about two-thirds of them are, in turn, teaching in their churches and communities. One Centurion has even moved to South Africa and is in the process of inaugurating a similar program there.

Your work in the project Evangelicals and Catholics Together, has a very "Kuyperian" look. Did he influence you to embark upon this effort? Has his example encouraged you to stay at it these ten years?

I was greatly influenced by Kuyper in starting, with Richard John Neuhaus, a group called Evangelicals and Catholics Together and in pursuing it through years of theological discussion and exploration (and no small amount of controversy along the way). I was not fully aware of it at the time, but this is precisely what Kuyper did. Kuyper, though he was a strong Calvinist with profound theological differences with Rome, nonetheless formed alliances with Roman Catholics and, in fact, built a political party, a coalition of Evangelicals and Catholics, which was ultimately successful in taking over the government of the Netherlands. Kuyper argued strenuously that such efforts were not only permissible but necessary in order to advance our common worldview. Evangelicals and Catholics hold common convictions, based on their common confession of the Creed, and they must take their stand together against the world spirit of the age to advance a biblical worldview.

Do you see any signs that a Christian consensus on culture matters is beginning to emerge? Overall, would you say you are encouraged by the present state of Christian involvement in culture?

There are many signs that a Christian consensus on culture is beginning to emerge. It is always difficult to characterize anything as evangelical, because there are so many different streams that feed into what we call the evangelical movement in America. But clearly, with the exception of some marginal groups, there is a growing awareness of the need for Christians to see all of life through a biblical worldview. We have just completed a major teaching project with Rick Warren, which is being distributed throughout the churches in his "Purpose-Driven" network as well as through the ministry of BreakPoint and Prison Fellowship. I have been supplying materials to various groups within the evangelical movement, all of whom seem to share a common understanding of the need for cultural engagement. There is also a growing sophistication by which Christians no longer regard cultural engagement as simply battling over abortion or gay rights and other surface issues; rather, we are beginning to understand the root problem, the rise of naturalism and the emergence of a utilitarian view of ethics. These are very grave threats to the Judeo-Christian consensus, which has historically informed Western civilization.

What advice would you offer to readers to encourage them to take up the example of Kuyper—and Colson—and become more effective kingdom citizens in culture matters?

To be good kingdom citizens in today's culture requires Christians first of all to learn to think Christianly; that is, to use our minds to analyze what is happening around us, to learn to read the signs of the times, as the sons of Issachar did. It means that we are to look at the daily newspaper and compare what is being said against what the Bible teaches, and to develop habits of the mind whereby we challenge the assumptions of modern culture and apply biblical tests and create biblical proposals. It also means that we are to be working diligently to restore reason in a postmodern era that has rejected reason. Rodney Stark has written a brilliant book, *The Victory of Reason*, in which he clearly demonstrates that it was Christianity that preserved reason in the West, and it was reason that brought so many of the great cultural innovations and so much progress through two thousand years.

Finally, kingdom citizens today need to see the world as a mission field, not just for fulfilling the Great Commission and winning people to Christ, but for engaging culture by being salt and light, arguing for justice and righteousness in the public square. We are self-consciously to work to bring the blessings of God to show forth in all areas of life for all people. That will require a sharp break from the evangelical "cloisterism" of the day, in which we sit contented in our churches, enjoying our self-directed worship, and forgetting what is happening in our communities and our nation. I am convinced that, as we develop the Christian mind and begin to apply reason and discernment to the issues of the day, we will quite naturally begin to engage—and transform—the culture around us.

Questions for Study or Discussion

1. Kuyper and Colson have looked very hard and long to discover the connections between God, his revelation, his plan and purpose for creation, and the culture in which they live. Can you think of some ways you might begin to do this more consistently?
2. Take a moment to inventory your own cultural involvement at present. In how many different arenas or types of culture are you presently involved? How do you try to use that involvement for advancing the kingdom of God? How *might* you?
3. Both Kuyper and Colson stress the importance of careful preparation in beginning to deal with culture matters. What ideas, plans, or course of action are you thinking about in order to prepare yourself for better engaging culture as a Christian?
4. Does your church sponsor any training or other opportunities to become involved in culture matters? Can you think of any ways to enhance or expand those opportunities?
5. Review the goals you set for this study at the end of chapter 1. Are you making progress in achieving them?

The Prophetic Power of Culture

The Christian Cultural Legacy of Czeslaw Milosz

And certainly a poet is almost always a revolutionary; I, for one,
believe so. A revolutionary who like other men lacks liberty, but with
the difference that he cannot accept his privation, and dashes against
the walls of his prison.

Luis Cernuda

Hear this, all peoples! Give ear, all inhabitants of the world, both low
and high, rich and poor together! My mouth shall speak wisdom; the
meditation of my heart shall be understanding. I will incline my ear to
a proverb; I will solve my riddle to the music of the lyre.

Psalm 49:1–4

CHRISTIANS TODAY FIND themselves frequently on the defensive when it comes to culture matters. There is no shortage of innovators and promoters of new forms and approaches to culture among those beyond the pale of faith. Each new season of fashion or television programming pushes the envelope of decency a little further. Promoters of values and practices that break from traditional morality seek new inroads into homes and schools, and new legitimacy through courts and legislatures. Pop culture continually creates new twists in language and encourages greater declines in civility, as a Gresham's Law of culture marginalizes traditional cultural forms, values, and norms more and more. The culture of the world leaches its way to respectability in the homes and churches of the land, where no effective cultural critique exists, little in the way of distinctly Christian culture is being produced, hardly any effective education in culture matters is available, and few exemplars stand out to lead the way to a Christian consensus on culture matters. Concerned church leaders and frightened parents scramble to circle the wagons against the pernicious, approaching enemy bearing down on them and their families. In an effort to defend themselves and their families against culture, many vilify whole segments of culture and thus forfeit an important arena of what Kuyper insisted was the Lord's turf and domain.

If there is one lesson to be learned from this, it is that culture can be an effective tool for advancing one's worldview. Culture can have a powerful prophetic role, as the prophets of secular culture demonstrate time and again. And this is all the more reason for contemporary Christians to strive for a consensus in culture matters: to create and promote forms and vehicles of culture that can penetrate the darkness of unbelieving worldviews and establish new inroads and beachheads for the gospel of grace. If unbelieving culture heralds and advances unbelieving worldviews, why should not distinctly Christian forms of culture be able to do the same?

Contemporary poetry provides an excellent example of the opportunity for prophetic cultural engagement from within the Christian community.[1]

The State of Contemporary Poetry

"It's true that what is morbid is highly valued today . . ."[2]

Many share the view held by the late Czeslaw Milosz, that poetry today has succumbed to a state of morbidity, "psychologically unhealthy . . . subject to or excessively concerned with unwholesome matters," as Webster's New College Dictionary explains this term. While there are yet many excellent poets producing works of true beauty—one thinks of Richard Wilbur, Seamus Heaney, Mary Oliver, X. J. Kennedy, Billy Collins, and Jane Hirshfield, among others—the vast majority of contemporary verse leaves much to be desired. Enthralled with the acclaim heaped on such masters of free forms, psychological introspection, and bold images as Walt Whitman, Sylvia Plath, and Allen Ginsberg; exhilarated by a feeling of liberation from all traditions, and stuck in a rut of institutionalization,[3] contemporary poets seem to wallow in a mire of formlessness, obscurantism, vulgarity, and mere subjectivity. As Joy Sawyer observes, commenting on contemporary verse, "Sometimes poetry seems incomprehensible, unobtainable, almost like a foreign language. Its often obscure meanings and strange speech can be intimidating."[4] Angst-ridden, angry, and accessible only to the cognoscenti of the contemporary literary scene, poetry today, as Dana Gioia points out,[5] is ignored by the vast majority of readers, including the members of the Christian community, for whom it is uninteresting, devoid of hope or joy, neurotic, and not particularly enjoyable to read.

Such poetry heralds a worldview of elitism, subjectivism, sensuality, and the trivialization of truth. While few today read poetry, those who do—and those who publish it—have all but cleared the decks of traditional forms and themes, and, along with those forms and themes, much in the way of appreciation for the great poetic masters and themes of the past. Poetry journals and books today are filled with the formless musings, eccentric introspections, and arcane images of modern and postmodern verse. Only a small elite engages the conversation.

The result is that, with but a few exceptions, Christians today have abandoned the field of poetry to the harpies and double-speaking prophets of contemporary verse. Here the Christian community is not even on the defensive against the encroaching worldviews of modernity and postmodernity. We have abandoned the hill altogether.

For most readers today, poetry is a waste of time. Certainly not all contemporary poetry falls into this category, however, and it is refreshing to encounter the occasional gem in the slag pile. When such a shining gem is a Christian work of art, we realize the power of culture to penetrate the darkness of our age in flight from God with the goodness, beauty, and truth of God. We learn that culture can be a valuable prophetic voice in an age abounding in false prophets.

Among such gems, the Lithuanian-born Polish/American poet Czeslaw Milosz, who died in August 2004, at the age of ninety-three, stood as a prophet in the wasteland, crying out in all his verse a message of Christian truth and hope in a clear and compelling voice. The

1980 Nobel Laureate is roundly regarded as one of the greatest poets of the last century. His work has found its way into virtually every well-known journal and magazine—either the poems themselves or reviews of his work by others. The encomia following his death came from all quarters, Christian and non-Christian, conservative and liberal, traditional and modern. While he may not have been a household name—in this country, that is; he was revered in Poland—Czeslaw Milosz projected a clear and powerful Christian voice into the world of contemporary letters. His verse stabbed the light of truth into the darkness of unbelief, and caused a world enamored of its secularity to hear again the ancient, "Thus saith the Lord."

Czeslaw Milosz: Background and Poetry

Czeslaw Milosz provides an excellent example of how the various forms of culture can serve as vehicles for truth. His achievement reminds us of why culture matters and can encourage and guide us as we seek a more thoughtful approach to it. In this chapter we will examine the poetry of Czeslaw Milosz, looking for lessons that we can apply to the task of achieving a Christian consensus on culture matters. And we'll consider the work of one contemporary Christian artist who, like Milosz, understands the prophetic power of culture and is using his chosen cultural form to wake up Christians and non-Christians alike to the power of truth.

Calling, background, and poetry

Milosz described himself as being "revolted against the craziness one observes today in art and literature and which reflects a more general madness."[6] Into the darkness of contemporary culture he resolved to project the knowledge of God and his glory, as seen from his unique vantage point on the world. Milosz's sense of calling in the work of poetry is aptly summarized in his poem "The Blacksmith Shop." Here, after reveling in bellows, blazing fire, molten iron, the sound of a beating hammer and sizzling steam, and the anticipation of horses waiting to be shod, Milosz concludes, "It seems I was called for this:/To glorify things just because they are."[7] It is a calling to which he was faithful for the better part of a century, and concerning which he prayed, as he entered his ninetieth year, "Give me certainty that I toiled for Your glory."[8]

Czeslaw Milosz was born in 1911 and raised in the village of Wilno, Lithuania. Many of his poems reflect on his earliest childhood memories. In the 1930s he moved to Paris, where he studied with a relative, Oscar Milosz, to whom he freely acknowledges his debt, both for his literary success and his worldview.[9] In Paris he first began to find his own poetic voice. Milosz moved to Warsaw before World War II and resided there throughout that conflagration. During the German occupation of Poland, he witnessed the madness of modernity, as well as the tragedy and heroism of his neighbors. After the war he served in the Polish government until becoming disillusioned with Marxism in the late 1940s. He defected to the West in 1951 and came to the attention of the American literary scene with his essay *The Captive Mind*,[10] a scathing analysis of the effects of Marxism on free intellectual thought. In 1961 Milosz became a professor at Berkeley, and he continued to live there for part of each year, alternating between Poland and his adopted country until his last days. In 1980 Milosz won the Nobel Prize for Literature. Thereafter, he continued to be a strong and active voice in contemporary poetry, publishing more than twenty-five books of verse, essays, letters, and diaries.

Milosz's subjects are varied and easy to grasp: childhood experiences; memories of friends and family; reflections on nature, cities, and places in general; philosophical and theological concepts; ekphrastic themes (poetry about art and works of art); dreams, imaginary vistas, and vignettes; and wartime experiences. In all such things he found abundant reason to reflect on matters transcendent and to raise a voice of wonder, praise, or thanks to God. While the forms of his poetry, at least in English translation, would be described as essentially free, they are consistent and even in each of his poems, which are carefully structured to let the main themes stand out clearly. His images are sharp, intimately described, and often disturbing; and one is aware, while reading Milosz, of his deliberate craftsmanship, structural integrity, and sense of timing, as well as of his intense desire to be understood by the reader.

A Christian voice

The feature that principally sets Milosz off from the vast majority of his peers is the pervasive presence of Christian themes in his verse. These themes are at times unmistakably overt, while at other times they lie beneath the surface of his poems and must be discerned in the brighter light of his entire *oeuvre*. Milosz's Roman Catholic faith was in many ways the driving force of his verse, and, while he never resolved all his doubts, and frequently allowed his spiritual musings to wander off the path of orthodoxy, there can be no doubt that here is a man whose contribution to culture reflects an essentially Christian view of life. Milosz wrote self-consciously of his sense of spiritual calling in the work of poetry. In a letter to Thomas Merton he wrote,

> In my poetry, in my readings (except professional readings in Slavic literature) I am preoccupied with religious problems and I strive hard. . . . My poetry has always been religious in a deeper sense, sometimes openly metaphysical, as in my long poem, "The World" written during the war.[11]

He acknowledged that "few people suspect my basically religious interests" but delighted that this situation "strategically, is perhaps better."[12] He may have meant by this that, were his religious themes not so subtle, were they more blatant, he might not have realized the wide readership and literary acclaim he enjoyed following his defection to the West. Milosz did not set out to be a "Christian poet." In the prose poem "It Appears," Milosz testifies that "the religious content of my poems is not the result of design by a believer; it grew out of my doubts, turmoil, and despair, as they searched for a form."[13] At the same time, it is clear that he felt called to this stance, and from early on in his career. He mused on this, albeit with some reluctance, in his poem "Capri," in which he identified the hand of Providence as "Might":

> Early we receive a call, yet it remains incomprehensible, and only later do we discover how obedient we were . . .

> Who will dare to say: I was called and that's the reason Might protected me from bullets ripping up the sand close by me, or drawing patterns on the wall above my head.[14]

In "Prayer" he testified to that same sense of divine calling on his life:

> I am ashamed, for I must believe you protected me,
> As if I had for You some particular merit.[15]

His sense of poetry as a divine calling is clear; however, his integration of faith into his observations and craft is not always immediately apparent. One has to read widely and carefully to see that Milosz is commenting on the world of the twentieth century from the perspective of one committed to the service of God. Yet his commitment to this calling is clear enough, and we may discern six aspects of his approach to carrying it out. Taken together these six aspects reveal Milosz to be a prophetic voice amid the wasteland of twentieth-century verse.

Understanding and assessing the modern dilemma

First, Milosz's Christian approach to poetry involves an effort to understand and assess the modern dilemma. Like Augustine, he knew that he had to offer a critique of the culture of his day before he would be able to justify his alternative, Christian view. He wrote as one who knew the importance of "understanding the times" (1 Chron. 12:32). A great deal of his poetry reflects on the madness and decadence of the modern world, a world that took reason and technology as its deity and left off the worship of the true God. Milosz comments broadly on the failure of the modernist experiment, a condition he captured succinctly in his poem "*Oeconomia Divina*":

> Roads on concrete pillars, cities of glass and cast iron,
> airfields larger than tribal dominions
> suddenly ran short of their essence and disintegrated.
> Not in a dream but really, for, subtracted from themselves,
> they could only hold on as do things which should not last.[16]

The failure of the modernist experiment, and of the prophetic or elucidating voice of modern poetry, is a primary theme of *The Witness of Poetry*, the Charles Eliot Norton Lectures at Harvard for 1981–82. Modernism and modern poetry failed because they turned their backs on transcendent reality, thus cutting off the human family from everything that gives meaning to existence, as well as from one another. When poetry, which should have maintained an eschatological and transcendent focus, turned its attention to merely secular and human themes instead, it lapsed into despair, which accounts for the "somber tone" of so much modern verse. As a mirror of and witness to its times, modern poetry failed in its mission, and has failed mankind as a result: "the weakening of faith in the existence of objective reality situated beyond our perceptions seems to be the cause of the malaise so common in modern poetry, which senses something like the loss of its raison d'être."[17]

Dedication to art

As a second aspect of his calling, Milosz was careful to remember that he was an artist, and not a preacher, as he stepped into the void created by the failure of modern verse. Thus, he remained conscious of the need to master the gift of language and to strive for beauty, goodness, and truth in his art. In this respect he recalls the Celtic Christian artists who gave such diligent attention to craft in their work. Nowhere is this obligation stated more beautifully than in the "Preface" to his *Treatise on Poetry*:

> First, plain speech in the mother tongue.
> Hearing it, you should be able to see
> Apple trees, a river, the bend of a road
> As if in a flash of summer lightning.
>
> And it should contain more than images.
> It has been lured by singsong,
> A daydream, melody. Defenseless,
> It was bypassed by the sharp, dry world.
>
> You often ask yourself why you feel shame
> Whenever you look through a book of poetry.
> As if the author, for reasons unclear to you,
> Addressed the worst side of your nature,
> Pushing aside thought, cheating thought.
>
> Seasoned with jokes, clowning, satire,
> Poetry still knows how to please.
> Then its excellence is much to be admired.
> But the grave combats where life is at stake
> Are fought in prose. It was not always so.
>
> And our regret has remained unconfessed.
> Novels and essays serve but will not last.
> One clear stanza can take more weight
> Than a whole wagon load of elaborate prose.[18]

Those last two lines leave us with no doubt about Milosz's intent as an artist. He was determined to use poetry as a vehicle for reflecting deeply on the "grave combats" of life. He intended his verse to serve a prophetic function, bringing the "weight" of glory to bear against the lightness of contemporary being.

A similar idea appears in the poem *"Ars Poetica?"* Here are the final two stanzas:

> The purpose of poetry is to remind us
> how difficult it is to remain just one person,
> for our house is open, there are no keys in the doors,
> and invisible guests come in and out at will.
>
> What I'm saying here is not, I agree, poetry,
> as poems should be written rarely and reluctantly,
> under unbearable duress and only with the hope
> that good spirits, not evil ones, choose us for their instrument.[19]

Milosz's poetry thus takes on the burden of pointing to transcendent truth by seeking to discern goodness and beauty in the midst of a fallen world, holding out, in carefully crafted lines and images, a message of hope amid the brokenness and despair of modernity. Whereas a preacher would cite scriptural chapter and verse to make his point, Milosz appealed to the kinds of experiences that modern and postmodern men and women have in common, leading them to reflect deeply as they take delight in the beauty and hopefulness of his verse. At the same time they are compelled to introspect concerning their own experiences of hopelessness and despair, and to wonder whether some hope might be found from beyond this mundane sphere.

A sense of gratitude

In the third place, Milosz approached his calling out of a deep sense of gratitude, motivated in his service to God and mankind by a profound thankfulness for the everyday blessings of life. He wrote to Thomas Merton: "My state of mind is that of a great gratitude to God for everything, for many miraculous happenings and narrow escapes."[20] Milosz expressed this sentiment powerfully in his poem "A Mistake":

> I thought: all this is only preparation
> For learning, at last, how to die.
> Mornings and dusks, in the grass under a maple
> Laura sleeping without pants, on a headrest of raspberries,
> While Filon, happy, washes himself in the stream.
> Mornings and years. Every glass of wine,

Laura, and the sea, land, and archipelago
Bring us nearer, I believed, to one aim
And should be used with a thought to that aim.

But a paraplegic in my street
Whom they move together with his chair
From shade to sunlight, sunlight into shade,
Looks at a cat, a leaf, the chrome steel on an auto,
And mumbles to himself, "*Beau temps, beau temps.*"

It is true. We have a beautiful time
As long as time is time at all.[21]

Rather than wallow in existential despair or mere outrage at tragic circumstances, Milosz looked for something to give thanks for, since he knew from experience that life can always be much worse. God has richly blessed us in the simplest things, but we are often too busy to pause, look or listen carefully, and reflect deeply on the loving kindness of the Lord all around us. Dietrich Bonhoeffer wrote of the importance of learning to give thanks for the little things in life, a practice much neglected by contemporary Christians:

Only he who gives thanks for the little things receives the big things. We prevent God from giving us the great spiritual gifts He has in store for us, because we do not give thanks for daily gifts. . . . We pray for the big things and forget to give thanks for the ordinary, small (and yet really not small) gifts. How can God entrust great things to one who will not thankfully receive from Him the little things?[22]

How, indeed? Milosz's poetry can help us to overcome this sad neglect of gratitude.

Clear communication

Fourth, Milosz testified to the need to work hard in order to communicate clearly. This conviction is diametrically opposed to much of modern verse, which often seems to revel in the obscure, arcane, and strictly subjective. He wrote to Thomas Merton, "I realize that nothing is more important than to find a common language with those who 'search in despair,' through poetry, prose, any means."[23] Here is how he expressed this conviction in the poem "In Common":

What is good? Garlic. A leg of lamb on a spit.
Wine with a view of boats rocking in a cove.
A starry sky in August. A rest on a mountain peak.

What is good? After a long drive water in a pool and a sauna.
Lovemaking and falling asleep, embraced, your legs touching hers.
Mist in the morning, translucent, announcing a sunny day.

I am submerged in everything that is common to us, the living.
Experiencing this earth for them, in my flesh.
Walking past the vague outline of skyscrapers? anti-temples?
In valleys of beautiful, though poisoned, rivers.[24]

Here we can see the ingredients of Milosz's poetry: Everyday images of simple human pleasures, the beauty of creation, relationships,
work, and the prospect of the future, set in precise forms against the
backdrop of a failed modernism and the tragedy of sin. One need not
have grown up in Lithuania or survived the war in order to identify
with such poignant images.

If, as Karl Shapiro has written, the only law of art "is that the
work must be capable of apprehension as a whole and at once,"[25]
then the poetry of Czeslaw Milosz certainly satisfies that requirement.
Here is poetry that one can immediately grasp, enter into, learn from,
and enjoy without becoming frustrated over impenetrable or illogical
images or complex language games.

Holding out hope

Fifth, like the great prophets of the Old Testament, Milosz considered an important aspect of his calling to be that of holding out
hope for the world. As he wrote in *The Witness of Poetry*,

> The world exists objectively, despite the shapes in which it appears in
> the mind and despite the colors, bright or dark, lent it by the happiness
> or misfortune of a particular man. That objective world can be seen as
> it is; yet we may surmise that it can be seen with perfect impartiality
> only by God. . . . The poet therefore appears as a man in love with the
> world, but he is condemned to eternal insatiability because he wants
> his words to penetrate the very core of reality. He hopes constantly
> and is constantly rejected.[26]

The message of hope is unmistakably clear in many of his poems, as
in "Hope": "Some people say we should not trust our eyes, / That there

is nothing, just a seeming, / These are the ones who have no hope."[27] Hope inheres in the simple things of life, the everyday situations and events where one may realize glimpses of glory. In "A Certain Poet" he wrote, "And yet what depth in those stanzas where, encoded, the most ordinary human dramas glow with a glare of ultimate things, what force in the transformation of the very stuff of people's everyday life into that marvelously muscular body of verse!"[28] But nowhere does the message of hope come across more clearly than in a section of the autobiographical "Diary of a Naturalist":

> My generation was lost. Cities too. And nations.
> But all this a little later. Meanwhile, in the window, a swallow
> Performs its rite of the second. That boy, does he already suspect
> That beauty is always elsewhere and always elusive?
> Now he sees his homeland. At the time of the second mowing.
> Roads winding uphill and down. Pine groves. Lakes.
> An overcast sky with one slanting ray.
> And everywhere men with scythes, in shirts of unbleached linen
> And the dark-blue trousers that were common in the province.
> He sees what I see even now. Oh but he was clever,
> Attentive, as if things were instantly changed by memory.
> Riding in a cart, he looked back to retain as much as possible.
> Which means he knew what was needed for some ultimate moment
> When he would compose from fragments a world perfect at last.[29]

Milosz hoped for a better world than what he lived through in the twentieth century, and he used his verse, at least in part, to "compose from fragments" a vision of what that world could be like. He sought to nurture the hope that, by returning to a vision of life under God, men and women could once again find reasons to give thanks. In Milosz's poetry, this hope is grounded not in the prospects of secular triumphalism or the murky and unstable abysses of the self, but in the transcendent reality of God and God's good and perfect plan for humankind. By cultivating a transcendent vision and looking at everyday realities in the light of that vision, Milosz believed that we can learn to rest in the often inscrutable goodness of Providence, and hope, despite our pain, that his good purposes will finally prevail.

Pursuing faithfulness

Finally, Milosz was determined in his approach to poetry to be content, not with succeeding at his calling, but with pursuing it faithfully all his days. God has not called us to be prosperous or famous, only faithful (1 Cor. 4:1–18). No matter what our station in life, or which aspects of culture come into our hands, this is a goal each of us can embrace. For Milosz, this meant being faithful in his verse. We get a glimpse of this devotion to faithfulness in the prose poem "To Wash":

> At the end of his life, a poet thinks: I have plunged into so many of the obsessions and stupid ideas of my epoch! It would be necessary to put me in a bathtub and scrub me till all that dirt was washed away. And yet only because of that dirt could I be a poet of the twentieth century, and perhaps the Good Lord wanted it, so that I was of use to Him.[30]

Balance this with the sense of resignation expressed in "One More Contradiction":

> Did I fulfill what I had to, here, on earth?
> I was a guest in a house under white clouds
> Where rivers flow and grasses renew themselves.
> So what if I were called, if I was hardly aware.
> The next time early I would search for wisdom.
> I would not pretend I could be just like others:
> Only evil and suffering come from that.
> Renouncing, I would choose the fate of obedience.
> I would suppress my wolf's eye and greedy throat.
> A resident of some cloister floating in the air
> With a view on the cities glowing below,
> Or onto a stream, a bridge and old cedars,
> I would give myself to one task only
> Which then, however, could not be accomplished.[31]

These six essential attitudes or convictions characterize Milosz's approach to fulfilling his calling as a poet writing from a Christian perspective. The Christian beliefs Milosz expressed are represented consistently, both in the more overtly Christian poems ("Theodicy," "Readings," "Why Religion?" "Lessons," "On Prayer," "At a Certain Age," "Prayer," etc.) and in those poems in which the message is more implicit and subdued ("Rivers Grow Small," "Abode," "This World," "In Her Diary," etc.). Reading his poetry, one is never very far from some ultimate question, for the answer to which Milosz consistently pointed away from the fading, troubled world to abiding, transcendent truths.

Here is an example of what I would describe as Milosz's explicitly Christian verse. In "Temptation," Milosz revealed his own bouts with meaninglessness and called on the name of the Lord to help him find the way of escape (lines 5–10 should be read as desolation's sermon to him):

> Under a starry sky I was taking a walk.
> On a ridge overlooking neon cities,
> With my companion, the spirit of desolation,
> Who was running around and sermonizing,
> Saying that I was not necessary, for if not I, then someone else
> Would be walking here, trying to understand his age.
> Had I died long ago nothing would have changed.
> The same stars, cities, and countries
> Would have been seen with other eyes.
> The world in its labors would go on as they do.
>
> For Christ's sake, get away from me.
> You've tormented me enough, I said.
> It's not up to me to judge the calling of men.
> And my merits, if any, I won't know anyway.[32]

Here again we can see Milosz's renunciation of anything like success or fame and his contentment to press on in his calling without regard for whether his work changes the world. The last line seems to point beyond time to eternity, where the poet will be occupied with more important things than whether he amounted to anything during his time on earth.

As an example of how Milosz's Christian message is implicitly communicated, consider "This World":

> It appears that it was all a misunderstanding.
> What was only a trial run was taken seriously.
> The rivers will return to their beginnings.
> The wind will cease in its turning about.
> Trees instead of budding will bend to their roots.
> Old men will chase a ball, a glance in the mirror—
> They are children again.
> The dead will wake up, not comprehending.
> Till everything that happened has unhappened.
> What a relief! Breathe freely, you who suffered much.[33]

Here there are no explicitly Christian themes, only subtle allusions to the worldview of the Bible: references to Ecclesiastes 1 (lines 3 and 4), the hope of new life and resurrection (lines 5–7), and the belief in a better life beyond death (lines 8–10). Milosz gently castigates the modernist world view, which failed to look beyond the present existence to the prospect of a better world (lines 1 and 2), and looks forward to a new beginning for those "who suffered much." Readers not steeped in a Christian worldview will doubtless find this poem appealing, yet enigmatic; they cannot fail to see the message of hope Milosz conveys. On the other hand, the Christian reader will be affirmed in his transcendent hope and comforted at the loss of those who suffered for their faith at the hands of those who cling too tightly to this world.

Lessons and Applications

The poetry of Czeslaw Milosz has much to offer contemporary Christians as we explore achieving consensus on culture matters. I want to suggest, in the first place, ways his poetry can help aspiring Christian poets, who could play a major role in forging such a consensus. Then I will turn to consider how others of the Christian community might benefit in this regard from reading.

Milosz's poetic vision should be a source of much encouragement for poets seeking to approach their craft from a distinctly Christian point of view. Six lessons come out of his experience and achievement as a religious poet in a secular century, a voice crying in the wilderness in the wasteland of modern verse.

The message of transcendent truth

First, it is clear from Milosz's achievement that modern/postmodern men and women are certainly open to the message of transcendent truth. The Christian poet, as poets such as Joyce Sutphen, Scott Cairns, Richard Wilbur, Wendell Berry, and Dana Gioia have shown, need not despair of not being able to communicate something of eternal substance to our unbelieving contemporaries. Poetry like that of Czeslaw Milosz, rich in familiar images and crafted with an attention to definite structure, clear and careful language, and impeccable timing, can grab the attention of modern readers and find a welcome reception. Christian poets should not confine their work merely to rehashing familiar Christian themes for the few Christian readers who might stumble across their verse. Rather, they should boldly launch the message of transcendent truth into contemporary secular arenas—through journals, readings, and Internet postings—in the confidence that unbelieving readers will lend an open ear.

Everyday encounters and experiences

However, and second, poetry that is rooted in transcendent convictions can connect with modern and postmodern people only when it meets them at the point of their everyday encounters and experiences. The precedent for such an approach to Christian verse is surely the Incarnation, in which Christ came down among us, experienced our misery, spoke our language, and talked to us of heavenly realities in strikingly mundane terms. The Christian poet cannot expect contemporary readers to be able (or willing) to unravel mazes of biblical imagery or to comprehend declarations of overtly theological truth; rather, as in the parables of Jesus, everyday actualities must be made to serve the cause of heavenly realities in a message of gratitude and hope. By appealing to the common experiences of contemporary men and women, Christian poets may hope to gain an audience among readers of verse.

Question, propose, and persuade

As they do, third, Christian poets must not try to preach. Their duty is to question, propose, and persuade. By leading the contemporary reader into everyday situations and experiences, and holding out the prospect of hope in a world as God sees and intends it, Christian poets can create a space for themselves at the table of contemporary literary conversation. They can do this by inviting the reader to consider the mundane from a new perspective, the perspective of the eternal and unchanging God. Christian poets need not insist on the absoluteness of their views; rather, using a self-critical and non-confrontational approach, they may, through images, questions, and the mind-set of a "fellow traveler," open up a dialogue with contemporary readers in which the possibilities of a Christian view of reality may at some point come into focus. Milosz managed this achievement wonderfully, as can be seen by reading any review of his poetry.

Hope not to convert, but to convert to hope

Fourth, Christian poets may not hope to convert their readers, but they may strive to convert them to hope. Poetry is not preaching; yet, in the hands of a Christian poet, it must not deny its role in holding out the good news concerning life as Christianity proclaims it. In this light, Christian poetry aimed at secular audiences is probably best seen as a tool of "pre-evangelism" rather than evangelism, serving to break up the hard ground of the secular heart in order to prepare it for the sowing of the gospel by more traditional methods. Few—doubtless, very few—will come to faith in God through reading Christian verse. At the same time, the consistent message of hope and the prospect of a transcendent world may enable some readers to find a way out of their morbidity and despair into a quest for lasting truth. This in itself would be a major contribution of contemporary Christian verse to our modern/postmodern generation. As Michael Polanyi put it in another context,

> Yet where the metaphysical believer cannot hope to convince, he may still strive to convert. Though powerless to argue with the nihilist he may yet succeed in conveying to him the intimation of a mental satisfaction which he is lacking; and this intimation may start in him a process of conversion.[34]

A transcendent metanarrative

Fifth, Christian poets must be bold to address the "big questions" of life, suggesting, as they do, the continuing existence of a transcendent metanarrative that makes sense of all our experience. Poetry that is satisfied simply to observe or to describe what is merely personal can end up being trivial. It is likely to leave the reader feeling, "Well, that's nice for you." Serious Christian poetry will engage the reader at the level of everyday experience and lead him or her to consider loftier matters through the careful use of structure, image, timing, and all the other poetic devices. Such poetry will be confident, visionary, forthright, honest, and critical of itself and its times; it will also communicate a tone of understanding, compassion, and peace.

Speak faithfully

Finally, the Christian poet must be content with faithfully seeking to speak transcendent truth into the world—"to compose from frag-

ments a world perfect at last"—without having to generate legions
of followers or converts as proof of artistic success. Christian poets
desiring to speak a word of truth to the contemporary generation must
see themselves as voices crying in the wilderness. As such, they may
be regarded by contemporary readers as strange, quaint, outdated,
irrelevant, or hopelessly naive. At the same time, if they work hard
to master their craft and strive through all the artistic means at their
disposal to connect with their contemporaries at the level of their
everyday experiences, they may expect to gain a hearing for transcendent truths and a message of gratitude and hope. And this should be
enough of a reward for their faithfulness.

Applications for Christians in culture matters

Christians who are not poets, but who give themselves to reading
and studying Milosz's poetry, will find that it can benefit their own
involvement in culture matters in at least three ways.

First, they will no doubt be persuaded that the various forms of
culture can be effective vehicles for tackling the "big issues" of life.
They will be startled, if not amazed, to discover how many important
themes can be addressed, assessed, and resolved, if only tentatively,
within the divine scheme of things in just a few brief lines of verse.
This may help to encourage them to seek more such insights in the
poetry of other writers from the Christian heritage of verse, to think
more deeply about the great issues and events of our own day, and
to consider ways their own involvement in culture matters might
similarly be used to proclaim a biblical perspective on life. Milosz's
poetry represents the kind of worldview thinking that many voices
are calling for today. As such, it can stretch our minds, broaden the
horizons of our vision, and teach us to live more completely and
consistently under the cope of heaven. And it can encourage us to
employ our own resources of culture—our homes, work, artistic tastes,
diversions, and conversations—for the purposes of God's kingdom.

Second, I find Milosz's poetry wonderfully entertaining and deeply
challenging. I would rather spend an evening mulling over a handful of
his verses than sit glued to the television set watching some rehashed
theme or situation. His poetry paints pictures in my mind that challenge my imagination to wander over landscapes, cityscapes, and the
everyday objects of life with new appreciation and delight. Like the
parables of Jesus, Milosz's verse encourages the reader to look more
closely and think more deeply about the simple things around us,

and enables us to bring greater delight into our everyday experience. He teaches us how to look at the world and see the purposes of God in created reality. Milosz gloriously fulfills what Natalie Goldberg has called "the writer's job," "to make the ordinary come alive, to awaken ourselves to the specialness of simply being."[35] Milosz can be for Christian readers a tutor in learning how to perceive the hand of God in the works of God, and thus to help others see it as well. He can provide an important part of our schooling to become what I have elsewhere described as "docents of glory."[36]

Finally, Milosz reminds all of us that the postmodern world is open for business when it comes to talking about spiritual matters. And he helps us see that culture, in any and all its forms, can be a potent tool for engaging in dialogue with secular contemporaries over the great, transcendent realities of the kingdom of God. As the apostle Paul reminds us in Ephesians 5:3–11, we are called to be lights in a dark world, glowing with the brilliance of God's glory, and exposing the wickedness and futility of sin. We need all the help we can get to fulfill this calling. The Christian verse of Czeslaw Milosz can both equip and motivate us to greater faithfulness in talking with others about the truths of Christian faith, and helping them to see the hope of the gospel.

Milosz summarized his poetic vision as follows:

> Humanity will explore itself in the sense that it will search for reality purified, for the "color of eternity," in other words, for simple beauty. . . . This means that our growing despair because of the discrepancy between reality and the desire of our hearts would be healed, and the world which exists objectively—perhaps as it appears in the eyes of God, not as it is perceived by us, desiring and suffering—will be accepted with all its good and evil.[37]

Here is a vision that contemporary Christians can readily appreciate and that, following the example of Czeslaw Milosz, and looking at his singular achievement as a Christian poet, they may strive for with great satisfaction and hope.

Contemporary Exemplar: David Wilcox

I have already mentioned several Christian poets who today are using their chosen cultural form to project light into the darkness of today's world. Men and women like Wendell Berry, Dana Gioia, Joyce Sutphen, Richard Wilbur, and Scott Cairns have, like Milosz, demonstrated the power of poetry to overcome the communication gulf that exists between the Christian and non-Christian worlds, and to establish beachheads for truth through the vehicles of culture. And, as with Milosz, their example encourages us to strive for the same through our own cultural pursuits. How might we, for example, use our conversations with others, a night at the movies or the theater, or a walk through the woods, to discern the presence of God, hear the message of truth through some medium of culture or creation, and engage our friends in lively discussions of eternal matters?

In the world of contemporary Christian music, one must listen far and wide to discover any truly prophetic voice. Phil Keaggy serves this role quite well, as does a less well-known guitarist and lyricist, David Wilcox, the closest thing to a contemporary Asaph that I have found.[38]

Toward the end of his reign, as David was making preparation for the building of the temple, he appointed the Levite Asaph to lead the people in worship and to prophesy before the Lord with song (1 Chron. 25:1–2). Asaph was painfully effective at his calling. The same can be said about David Wilcox.

Like Asaph, Asheville's David Wilcox writes songs with deeply spiritual and powerfully convicting messages. Both men are, or were, prophets. Both impact or impacted audiences to the glory of God. But the comparison ends there. For Asaph, the biblical composer/prophet, was strictly to-the-point, no-holds-barred, and in-your-face. David Wilcox, by contrast, delivers a more winsome and subtle, though no less penetrating and convicting, message. Wilcox is a stealth prophet, an Asaph-under-the-Radar, whose lilting, good-times melodies carry blockbuster messages of spiritual insight, conviction, and hope in stories and musings on everyday events and things.

Aficionados of contemporary Christian rock receive no consideration from Wilcox. He knows they probably won't like his music—after all, where are the drums, synthesizers, and female back-ups?—but he doesn't care, as he makes clear in "Sex and Music." He is a man on a mission, and anyone who doesn't like him is free to tune in elsewhere. He is not interested in selling huge quantities of CDs; like Milosz, his passion is for honesty, truth, and a life lived faithfully and fully before the Lord. Wilcox's classy acoustical guitar and mellow baritone voice carry a message about everyday faith and what it means to live for Christ in a pop-culture, self-centered world that seems ever on the verge of self-destructing. He challenges his audiences to have fun but to pay attention; to reminisce but to repent; and to cut the nonsense and get on with the demands of faith for daily life.

Asaph, born too long ago to benefit from Emily Dickinson's advice to "tell the truth, but tell it slant," was as direct as a thrown brick in calling Solomon's generation to shake off its comfort and complacency and do serious business with God. The twelve psalms attributed to him (50, 73–83) are filled with dire warnings and calls to repent of sin and to return to the living God. David Wilcox's message is similar, but his approach is more Dickinsonian. His broad swipes at hypocrisy and shallowness reach all of us in the community of faith in one way or another.

Wilcox takes pop culture arm-in-arm and uses it to reveal our selfishness and insensitivity. We laugh all the way through "Moe," in which he recalls the abuse he suffered as a child because of his father's resemblance to a certain afternoon-TV buffoon. But perhaps we cry as well as we remember suffering similarly ourselves, or having inflicted such suffering mindlessly on others, who, through no fault of their own, presented convenient targets for our self-advancing ridicule.

Sin easily sneaks up on us, David Wilcox warns in "Slipping through My Fist." Temptation entices us to wonder, "What if . . . ?" as we give in to some small moral lapse, just to see where it might lead. Before we know it, we have drifted far from our moorings and are filled with remorse and regret for our loss. We should know better than to give in to the little sins. We ought to be more responsible with the frail vessel God has entrusted to our care.

We are responsible not only for ourselves in this brief time we have here, but for one another as well. It may be hard to confront another's sinfulness, Wilcox advises in "Guilty Either Way," but the costs are greater if we fail to do so. Better to run the risk of alienating a friend than to lose him or her to the tragic consequences of a life consumed by sin.

There's a positive point to Wilcox's focus on our foibles and folly. As he explains in "If It Wasn't for the Night," the dark times we experience in this life can serve to illuminate more brightly the grace of God. In this song Wilcox compares the coming of Christ amid the dark and dead of winter to the way spring gathers momentum under the snow, bursting forth in beauty when the time is right. Christ's coming to a world of darkness and sin encourages us to hope for renewal from even our deepest sin and despair.

God knows how to reach us right where we are, and this is part of the wonder and mystery of his grace. In "Native Tongue" Wilcox celebrates God's joy in gathering up the "scattered fragments" of our lives and using them to build bridges to himself. He heals us at the point of our brokenness and speaks our "native tongue" as he communicates his grace to needy and hurting sinners of all kinds. But coming to know God is not merely a psychological crutch; nor is it the result of rational argument. Knowing the Lord is a great mystery, and we need to allow that mystery to engulf and overwhelm us. In "Out of the Question" Wilcox counsels us not to try to box God into intellectual categories. He is too big and too mysterious for that, and we will know the sweet joy and assurance of a relationship with him only as we set aside our questions and settle into the mystery of God by faith alone.

Then we discover the real meaning of our fleeting lives. The useless materialism Wilcox decries in "Never Enough" must give way to a more spiritual focus if we truly want to live. In "Spirit Wind" Wilcox, returning from a funeral, contemplates a plastic bag lifted and carried along by a dust whirlwind. As the little twister plays out and the bag falls to earth, he is reminded of how fleeting life is, and that what finally matters is our ability to tap into the wind of God's eternal Spirit. We have been "made to fly" and must make the most of every "precious chance" to be carried along in the Spirit wind of God.

The people who worshipped under the leadership of Asaph probably got tired of his grating, indicting, threatening psalms. But the people of Hezekiah's day valued them and used them to seek the Lord in renewal and reformation (2 Chron. 29:30). David Wilcox is much more enjoyable to listen to, but his message is just as pointed and just as needed in our comfortable and complacent churches. By exploring the revelation of God in everyday situations and things, David Wilcox teaches us to examine ourselves and to listen for the voice of the Lord as he daily calls us to repentance and renewal. His melodies may be memorable and his lyrics fun, but don't let that lull you into comfort. This present-day Asaph-under-the-Radar shoots real bullets. Listen to his music with your friends—saved or unsaved—and let this prophetic cultural voice stimulate animated conversations about ultimate things. David Wilcox's music can not only serve as a vehicle for conversation about culture matters, but it can help to train us in the kind of insights, affections, and practices that are consistent with the biblical worldview we profess.

Questions for Study or Discussion

1. Have you read much poetry? Do you have a favorite poem, perhaps one you remember from childhood? What about that poem is memorable to you? Why?
2. Read back over the citations from the poetry of Czeslaw Milosz. Make a list of all the "everyday things" or experiences he mentions. How many of these have you ever encountered? Have they ever led you to think about God or his purpose for the world? Might they?
3. Remember the lessons from Milosz's poetry for our concern about culture matters: focus on truth, God in everyday things, propose and persuade, convert to hope, a transcendent metanarrative, faithfulness. Think of your own involvement in culture matters—your work, taste in music, television habits, and so on. Which of those six lessons might you apply directly to your situation? How might doing so affect your involvement in culture matters?
4. Milosz encourages us that culture can help us to see God and to communicate truth about him to our contemporaries, thus engaging a dialogue about the things that matter most in life. Do you have any experience doing this? Explain. Can you think of some ways you might begin to apply the lessons from Milosz's example in your own life?
5. Our secular and postmodern contemporaries are definitely "open for business" when it comes to talking about spiritual matters. Culture can be a powerful vehicle for building bridges along which conversations about ultimate things can travel. Why do you suppose more Christians are not actively involved in this pursuit? How can we overcome the obstacles keeping us from using culture as a prophetic tool in advancing the kingdom of God?

6

Toward a Christian Consensus

Recommendations for Individual Believers and Responsible Communities

If this is the conclusion of our study—that the problem of Christ and culture can and must come to an end only in a realm beyond all study in the free decisions of individual believers and responsible communities—it does not follow that it is not also our duty to attend to the ways in which other men have answered and answer the question, and to ask what reasoning accompanied their free, relative, and individual choices.

H. Richard Niebuhr

But seek first the kingdom of God and his righteousness, and all these things will be added to you.

Matthew 6:33

IN HIS LANDMARK 1951 book, *Christ and Culture*, H. Richard Niebuhr showed that the question of how Christians and Christianity must relate to the culture of their times is as old as the faith itself. In every generation Christians have wrestled with culture matters, yet we have not managed to achieve a common approach. How the followers of Christ should relate to the culture of their day is a perennial question precisely because it is so pressing and so perplexing. It seems almost naive to hope that some generation of Christians might be able to break the mold of all previous generations—which were, as is our own, divided by conflicting approaches to culture matters—and discover some common ground for a consensus on this important question.

Niebuhr argued that over the centuries, Christians have proposed five ways of dealing with culture matters: Christ in opposition to culture; Christ ennobling and fulfilling culture; Christ above culture, proffering a culture above culture; Christ and culture in tension; and Christ the transformer of culture. Each of these approaches has something worthwhile to contribute to a Christian approach to culture matters. And, with but a little variation, and some change in labeling, the approaches to culture outlined in the introduction to this present study are essentially the same as those identified by Niebuhr. We are simply, in our generation, carrying on the same debate concerning culture matters in which our forebears in the faith engaged. Like us, they made little progress toward a Christian consensus on culture matters, except within particular communions. Niebuhr wrote that the answer Christians give to the question of the relationship between Christ and culture is "unconcluded and inconclusive."[1] He insisted that the only consensus on culture matters any generation of believers might be able to achieve is the kind of "live and let live" approach summarized in the quotation that begins this final chapter: Individual believers and responsible communities must, after all has been studied, make free and relative decisions concerning how they will approach and engage the culture of their day; at the same time, they must be tolerant toward others whose approach differs from their own, and commit to the hard work of trying to understand their reasoning. Beyond that, at least as Niebuhr seemed to think, not much is to be hoped.

In Niebuhr's day the lines were rigidly drawn between Protestants, Catholics, and Orthodox; and the evangelical movement, the influence of which has been felt across the spectrum of Christian communities, was just struggling to be born. Since 1951 that movement has given birth to a variegated and cross-denominational parachurch enterprise, has spawned a thriving culture in media and higher education, and has sponsored and participated in the Lausanne Forum, which has opened up communications among evangelicals and other Christians on a worldwide scale. Further, the reforms of Vatican II and the pa-

pacy of John Paul II have helped to create an atmosphere of exciting dialogue with Roman Catholics, as embodied in such efforts as the movement known as Evangelicals and Catholics Together. The Orthodox writings of such theologians as Georges Florovsky, Alexander Schmemann, and D. G. Hart have found widespread acceptance in the Christian community as a whole. A greater appreciation of the ascetic life, which Orthodox and Catholic believers have always cherished, is more observable among all the communions of the church. And the Pentecostal movement, which has influenced both evangelical and Roman Catholic traditions, has gained greater respectability and acceptance with all Christians.

All of which is simply to note that things have changed since Niebuhr's day, when the possibility of a clearer and more compelling consensus on culture matters seemed unlikely, due to the constrictions within which the body of Christ existed in America and elsewhere. But with the growing openness of various communions to one another, the interdenominational and cross-denominational nature of so many different aspects of contemporary Christianity, and the existing dialogues and forums in which members of various communions are presently engaging with mutual love and respect—given all these developments, surely the time is ripe for pressing on beyond "live-and-let-live" to a greater consensus on culture matters than has heretofore existed in the church.

Niebuhr understood how important the question of our relationship to culture is, not only because of the nature of Christ and the kingdom of God, but because of the nature and inescapability of culture. He wrote,

What we have in view when we deal with Christ and culture is that total process of human activity to which now the name *culture*, now the name *civilization*, is applied in common speech. Culture is the "artificial, secondary environment" which men superimpose on the natural. It comprises language, habits, ideas, beliefs, customs, social organization, inherited artifacts, technical processes, and values. . . . Culture is the work of men's minds and hands. It is that portion of man's heritage in any place of time which has been given us designedly and laboriously by other men, not what has come to us via the mediation of nonhuman beings or through human beings insofar as they have acted without intention of results or without control of the process. Hence it includes speech, education, tradition, myth, science, art, philosophy, government, law, rite, beliefs, inventions, technologies.[2]

Culture matters, in other words; and, when it comes to culture matters, those who live in vital relation to the King and Lord of all cultures and kingdoms must not treat this as a subject of secondary importance. It involves all of life, all the time, and all our relationships, roles, and responsibilities. Furthermore, our approach to culture must be seen as an aspect of our pursuit of the kingdom of God, and decidedly subservient thereunto. Niebuhr wrote, at the end of his study, "the world of culture—man's achievement—exists within the world of grace."[3] The approach we take to engaging the culture of our day must be shaped by our citizenship in the kingdom of God; moreover, that approach will, whether we are conscious of it or not, give strong testimony to the watching world concerning the nature and importance of that eternal realm.

That being so, while we can certainly agree with Niebuhr as to the importance of each individual and each community of Christians coming to their own free decisions, after considered study of the question, and with a generous and tolerant spirit toward one another, still I am persuaded, especially in the light of a growing ecumenicity, that our common pursuit of the eternal kingdom of Christ can bring us further along toward a consensus on culture matters than simply agreeing to disagree. Not that we should expect all believers in any generation to agree at every point, or with every protocol, priority, or practice; rather, we might dare to hope that *parameters can be articulated and a variety of forums created to enable significant numbers of believers from all communions of the faithful to realize a common voice and stance toward the making and use of culture in all its forms.* This is the goal of a Christian consensus on culture matters.

In this last chapter, therefore, I want to point in the direction of such a consensus, first, by restating the conclusions from our study of previous generations of believers and their contemporary counterparts. What we have observed in our forebears, and seen illustrated by contemporary examples, suggests the broad outlines of what could become a Christian consensus on culture matters. I want to rephrase those observations in the form of a set of affirmations concerning a Christian approach to culture matters that can enable the present generation of the followers of Christ to accomplish the goal set forth in the preceding paragraph.

Getting to that consensus will require the conscientious effort of individual believers and responsible communities. Therefore, second, I want to recommend certain very specific activities—for individual believers and responsible communities—that are consistent with our calling to seek first the kingdom of God and his righteousness, and which, if faithfully pursued, can enhance our ecumenical endeavors and help to bring the family of Christ together in new and more effective ways with respect to culture matters.

Aspects of a Christian Consensus

This book has been an examination of various aspects of a Christian approach to culture matters that proved effective in their time for helping segments of the church pursue the kingdom of God and his righteousness amid the vicissitudes and uncertainties of contemporary culture. The elements we have examined, and which we will review in this section, have been present in the church, in one form or another, and to a greater or lesser extent, in virtually every age, although, as Niebuhr showed, without serving in any generation as an agreed-upon approach to culture matters. Taken together, these elements outline the parameters of an approach to culture matters that can promote consensus for the members of the body of Christ in its various communions. We might have considered many other individuals and times and come to the same five aspects of a Christian approach to culture matters. Ephraem the Syrian, in his hymns against the Emperor Julian, might have served as an example of cultural critique in the generation prior to Augustine, as Clement of Alexandria might have in the late second century, Savonarola in the fifteenth, or Francis Schaeffer in the late twentieth. The Renaissance culture of late medieval Italy and Germany, or the Dutch Calvinist culture of twentieth-century North America could have supplied examples, equally as excellent as the artists of the Celtic Christian period, of forging a distinctly Christian culture out of inherited traditions and the needs and opportunities of the day. The labor of late medieval monks and scholars in creating the cathedral schools and the first universities, or the pioneering educational works of Alcuin and Rabanus Maurus in the Carolingian period, could have served as well as Calvin's example to encourage us in taking up the work of educating ourselves for kingdom living. Instead of Kuyper as an example of broad cultural involvement we could have studied Basil, the fourth-century bishop of Caesarea, or William Wilberforce or Thomas Chalmers in nineteenth-century England. And, as an example of culture speaking to the church and penetrating the unbelieving world with prophetic power, instead of Milosz we might have considered the first Jesuit missionaries to North America, the abolitionist media of early nineteenth-century America, or the civil rights movement led by Dr. Martin Luther King Jr. The examples selected for this book are only the ones that have most engaged my interest over the years, and that seemed to me to hold real potential for directing us toward a Christian consensus on culture matters.

In this section, therefore, I propose to revisit those five aspects of a Christian approach to culture, phrasing them in the form of affirmations that, together, can outline a broad playing field for contemporary Christians to take up the work of culture matters according to a more clearly defined consensus. Along the way it will be seen that the following are not five distinct aspects; rather, they overlap, bleed into one another, depend on and derive from one another, and so are really part and parcel of a whole-cloth approach. Assuming that there is agreement, at least on the part of many readers, that the present state of division outlined in the introduction is unacceptable, the affirmations that follow, though they would not overcome all our differences, could nonetheless serve as rallying points for a more united front in the culture matters of our generation. Such a consensus would hopefully result in cultural engagement and endeavor more characteristic of the kingdom of God, and therefore, more conducive to its advancement, than is presently in evidence among the members of the body of Christ.

Sustain a comprehensive, timely, judicious, and broad-based critique of culture

There can be no distinctly Christian cultural activity apart from a concerted, ongoing critique of contemporary culture in all its forms. Like Augustine, and as the journal *First Things* illustrates, that critique must be comprehensive, timely, broad-based, fair, biblical, and evangelical, and it must involve representatives from across a broad spectrum of the Christian world. The kind of critique of culture we need must engage believers at all levels of the church with a view to challenging their unexamined assumptions concerning culture matters, quickening their interest in this subject, and shaping their involvement with culture in a manner more consistent with the kingdom of righteousness, peace, and joy in the Holy Spirit. Such a critique must take place via many media and in many settings—print, Internet, CD, seminars and courses, in Sunday schools and Bible study groups, from lecterns and pulpits, and in casual conversations among friends. It must take into consideration views from across the spectrum of the household of faith. And it must create opportunities for others to join in the discussion and make their contribution toward the new consensus.

Such a vibrant, broad-based, and timely critique will not simply happen; neither can we expect that any one journal, group, school, publishing house, or media outlet will be able to bring it into being. Each member of the community needs to ask hard questions about his or her responsibility in helping to create this critique and then in sustaining it through active participation. A lively and comprehensive Christian critique of culture is already under way, as I have previously mentioned. At present it is limited to a few periodicals, certain websites, a growing number of writers and speakers, and a handful of publishers and organizations. But the critique needs to be expanded and energetically introduced into those settings where the majority of Christians might expect to engage it; and those currently involved in this critique in isolation from one another need to seek ways of uniting their voices both to make the case to the whole church that culture matters, and to speak to a wide range of culture matters in the name of the kingdom of God.

Support the development of distinctly Christian cultural forms

At the same time, we must begin more energetically to encourage the development of distinctly Christian forms of culture, across the broad spectrum of cultural activities outlined by Niebuhr and suggested throughout the course of this study. Already an aggressive effort is being made to sustain a Christian pop culture in music and certain of the arts. Christians have also devoted a great deal of energy and resources to the creation of evangelistic and liturgical programming through radio and television, which represents a kind of Christian culture all its own. We can debate the effectiveness or even the validity of this cultural expression, but there can be no denying the reality of it. There have always been individual believers—such as Milosz, Flannery O'Connor, C. S. Lewis, and others—working in the field of literature; and there is a growing body of Christian scholars beginning to hold forth in Christian and secular institutions, as well as in professional societies, on behalf of distinctly Christian approaches to teaching, learning, and various disciplines of study. Christian artists also continue to produce high-quality works in the visual arts, and various expressions of Christian revolt against public education have created a culture of Christian education in homes, day schools, and classical schools. For many years a variety of individuals and institutions have labored to establish distinctly Christian approaches to marriage and family life, the nature and use of wealth, and Christian involvement in prisons and politics.

Although a great deal of activity is already under way, most Christians tend to be narrowly selective in their involvement in culture matters. Little in the way of a comprehensive philosophy of culture exists, and most of the activity summarized above is happening beyond the attention or the interest zones of the vast majority of believers, very often with precious little support from the community as a whole. Whole fields of cultural endeavor are yet to be explored.

Yet everyone is a creator of culture, as Paul Johnson argues.[4] We are always using and making culture, actively participating in a wide range of cultural activities, in all of which, even down to the mundane routines of table manners, Christians are called to be conscious of serving the interests of Christ, and to demonstrate the reality of the kingdom of glory (Col. 3:23; 1 Cor. 10:31). There are kingdom norms for how we speak and converse (Eph. 4:29–5:4; Col. 4:6); how we raise our children and manage our homes (Ps. 78:1–8; Eph. 6:1–4; 1 Peter 3:1–6); what we do with our wealth (Ps. 24:1; Matt. 25:14–30); how we carry on in our work (Col. 3:22–4:1; 1 Thess. 4:9–12); what we do with our time (Ps. 90:12; Eph. 5:15–17); and, indeed, for every form of cultural endeavor, whether mundane and popular or fine and selective. Taken together, these norms constitute a worldview, a prescription for living the reality of the kingdom of God in the everyday affairs of the whole of life, in all of culture. They provide the framework within which we might expect the Lord Jesus to fulfill our prayer that he would bring his kingdom to greater reality on earth, mirroring the way it presently exists in glorious beauty before him in heaven (Matt. 6:9–13).

Yet how much deliberate effort is actually evident in the churches of the body of Christ at studying, identifying, developing, and nurturing these cultural norms for every area of life in the kingdom of God? Or in encouraging and assisting those who are trying to identify those norms and bring them to expression in distinctly Christian cultural forms? The kingdom of God is our highest priority as believers;

culture, in all its forms, provides a wealth of resources, opportunities, and venues for advancing that reign of righteousness, peace, and joy in the Spirit. But this will occur only as we apply ourselves, throughout the Christian community, to the creation of distinctly Christian forms of culture for every area of our lives—everything from the arts and education to work, conversation, civility, wealth and its use, and marriage and family life. In all these areas there is much work to be done.

Take up the work of educating the church for kingdom living

This, in turn, leads to our third affirmation. The members of the body of Christ must accept the responsibility of learning to live the kingdom in every area of life, so that the righteousness, peace, and joy of that eternal realm will shine through in all our activities, including all our involvement with culture matters. Without such a renewed, community-wide educational commitment, the "kingdom of God" will continue to exist only within the walls of our churches, amid the programs we sponsor and in which we participate, and as little more than a niche of time, rather than the ever-present, all-subsuming, all-transforming reality Christ intends it to be.

Over the past two or three generations Christians have been educating themselves out of the mainstream of public life and to the margins of society, where they fidget and fuss over every personal woe, fiddling away in collective navel-gazing while the enemies of the kingdom burn down the house around us. We must begin to demand more of ourselves and of those who are seeking to form us in the truth of God. We must call for approaches to teaching and learning that will bring the reality of Christ's rule to open expression and vibrant life in and through all the cultural activities of our lives. This may lead us to scrap or retool certain educational sacred cows (is Sunday school as we know it really a fruitful endeavor?). It will cause us to challenge our long-cherished assumptions concerning what constitutes true learning (is it merely a subjective sense of well-being engendered by the experience of gaining some new insight on truth?). This call will encourage us to experiment with new approaches to teaching; to take more seriously the need to assess every aspect of our instruction; and to insist that those who take up the mantle of teaching devote themselves to ongoing learning consistent with a biblical worldview. We must challenge existing strongholds of Christian education to reassess their presuppositions and practices and modify their formats, curricula, and objectives accordingly (after all, the traditional seminaries, whose approach to education has remained largely unchanged since the 1940s, trained the leaders on whose watch the church has landed on the margins of society). And we must consider that, since the work of Christian formation is ultimately the responsibility of the Holy Spirit, all our efforts in teaching and learning must be constructed and pursued with a view to making wide room for him to work, according to his preferences, objectives, and methods.

I am writing these words as I participate in a conference on biblical worldview involving high school and college students in eastern North Carolina. The program was begun by Joe Wirtz as a result of his reading of Chuck Colson and Nancy Pearcey's book, *How Now Shall We Live?* Joe was in the first class of Centurions, where he gained greater vision and insight to help in shaping this very creative training program he sponsors each summer on the campus of North Carolina State University. Students participate in a rigorous period of preparatory reading, study, and discussion. At the conference they select a track providing opportunities to participate in political and legislative life, the production of a daily newspaper, or the creation of an original drama, while, at the same time, they continue to receive instruction by traditional means in worldview topics and join together for nightly worship. In every setting—seminars, plenary session, discussion groups, worship, working caucuses, team activities—adults are involved with students to wrestle with culture matters from the biblical perspective provided in their preliminary training and plenary sessions. Every day the students and their mentors have opportunity to observe the fruit of their learning in individual and group activities. Such a varied, intensive, and focused approach to teaching represents, I believe, the kind of educational change that needs to happen in the churches, where serious doctrinal and philosophical engagement, varied approaches to teaching and learning, a focus on cultural as well as spiritual life, and an emphasis on specific outcomes must replace our present "information-transfer/feel-OK" model of instruction. Unless we make radical changes in our approach to Christian formation, we shall not be able to sustain a lively critique of culture or to discover, embrace, and bring to expression the new Christian cultural forms, and the biblical worldview, that our Christian consensus on culture matters requires.

Nurture an appreciation for the cultural heritage and pioneers
of the Christian past

Part of that education must involve wide study in the pioneers
and heritage of Christian culture from the past. That such exemplars
and such a legacy of Christian cultural engagement exist will come
as a surprise to most members of the Christian community. So effective have been the secular accounts, the exhibitions at museums, the
courses in our schools, the shows on PBS, and the programs sponsored by secular institutions of higher culture at muting or denying
the distinctly Christian aspects of that heritage, that most believers
have little or no awareness of the kinds of creative Christian genius
that guided the arts in the past. And so consistent has been the present generation of Christian preachers and teachers at ignoring that
heritage that, were they even to be made aware of it, most Christians
would doubtless assume that it was unimportant to the life of faith
(after all, wouldn't my pastor have mentioned it?).

But the high-water marks of Western culture have their origins
within the community of faith. In virtually every field of cultural
endeavor Christians have played a leading role, discovering norms,
creating forms, and passing on their ideas and skills to others. The
development of Western art, music, literature, architecture, politics,
education, law, and economics—even such modern languages as English, German, Spanish, and French—is inconceivable apart from the
contributions of Christians, and the worldview they embodied, in
every age. Today the great cultural achievements of the Christians of
the past are held captive in secular museums, by secular symphony
societies and recording companies, and in the classrooms of secular
universities, where they are reinterpreted as little more than a stage
in the evolution of culture to its present, postmodern confusion. Yet
today's makers of culture have been very much aware of the achievement of our Christian forebears, and have learned from them, and
borrowed freely from their legacy: one thinks of Durer's influence
on the young Andrew Wyeth, the impact of Bach on the Beatles, the
example provided by the medieval guilds for the labor movement of
the early twentieth century, the role of Christianity in the formative
years of the scientific revolution, and the impact of John Witherspoon
on the separation of powers in the American Constitution. But believers today continue to ignore this heritage, which has the potential for
making a strong contribution to our consensus and to the development
of Christian forms of culture appropriate to our own day.

Here there is much grist to mill in reading and discussion groups and as part of the curriculum of Christian formation in churches, and much nourishment to be gained through teaching, preaching, and direct involvement—via recordings, museums, good conversation, and personal study. Much of what is good and useful in contemporary culture can be traced back to the minds and crafts of earlier generations of the followers of Christ. They have much to teach us still, and we owe them a debt of gratitude that we must not fail to acknowledge and satisfy.

Seek avenues for deploying the fruit of Christian culture in the world and for the world

Too often the discussion of biblical worldview and Christian culture takes the form of "us vs. them." "They" have ruined culture, and it is "our" duty to recover it for ourselves and our children (or, alternately, to avoid or condemn culture). "They" are hopelessly lost and depraved, while "we" know the truth and must insist on it whether "they" like it or not. "We" are accused by "them" of trying to impose "our" views, while "we" indict "them" for doing the same without acknowledging it. Instead of using our salt to excite flavor for Christian culture, we are rubbing it in the wounds of a failed secular order. Instead of letting our light glow with an attractive warmth and luminescence, we blare it in the face of a world that cannot endure the wattage we insist that it accept.

The reality is that the high Christian cultural tides of the past have raised all the ships in the harbor—those of the believing community and of the unbelievers as well. Can we erect our consensus to include the insistence that our culture, like the Lord who inspires it, promote goodness, beauty, and truth for every human being to enjoy? That it should speak prophetically to both the church and the world? Can we demonstrate the benefits to the entire community of forms of culture developed from distinctly Christian premises for distinctly Christian purposes? Shall we invite our unbelieving neighbors to share in this conversation with us? Can we avoid the smugness and cultural apartheid vis-à-vis our non-Christian neighbors that will certainly doom our project from the beginning? Will our distinctly Christian cultural forms be welcomed into secular venues because of their undeniable excellence and clarity? And will we send our brightest cultural lights to serve in the very hotbeds of unbelieving life and culture, after the example of Milosz and others? Let us hope that it might be so.

A consistent, broad-based critique; active creation and support of Christian cultural forms; education for kingdom living; appreciation of the heritage of Christian culture; cultural forms that speak prophetically to and benefit those both within and beyond the community of the redeemed: These five affirmations, taken as our objective, can serve as rallying points for a consensus on culture matters engaging the entire Christian community, guiding individual believers and responsible communities to take up the work required of them.

Guidelines for Individual Believers

It remains, therefore, to consider what individual believers and their communities can do to begin working toward the realization of such a Christian consensus on culture matters as outlined above. I will be brief, as these activities are largely self-evident and require but little explanation.

Become more culturally self-conscious

Reread the introduction to this book. Which of these approaches to culture matters most characterizes you? Which need to become more part of your own approach and practice? Begin paying attention to your own involvement with culture—what you read, wear, and eat; the subjects of your conversation, as well as your choice of words and expressions; what you watch on television; what films and music you indulge; your diversions and entertainments. What factors determine the nature of your involvement in such culture matters? Mere habit, or pragmatic conformity to peers? Simple pleasure or boredom? Professional or personal advancement? Thoughtful desire to further the interests of Christ's kingdom? Get in the habit of asking yourself, concerning any of your cultural activities or practices, "How is this helping to advance the kingdom of Christ and his righteousness?" Bring the work of prayer to bear on your involvement in culture matters. Let the presence of the kingdom—and its exalted King—intrude on your cultural interests and activities. By doing so you may discover areas of needed change, growing interest, or opportunity for growth and for glorifying God through culture matters that you have not previously recognized.

The Apostle Paul exhorts us to pay careful attention to how we conduct our lives in the world (Eph. 5:15–17). Presumably, this includes our involvement with culture matters. Let his words encourage us to pursue a more thoughtful and more consistently Christian approach to culture matters, and even to involve others with us in that pursuit.

Receive culture as a gift and a trust

Get in the habit of thinking of all your involvement in culture matters as part of your calling and trust from God. Thank him daily for the many expressions of culture with which he blesses you, including those that come from the unbelieving world (Ps. 68:18), and for every opportunity to use culture to advance his kingdom of righteousness, peace, and joy in the Spirit. Cherish as precious every aspect of culture in which you become involved (what you can't cherish, or feel skittish cherishing, you may need to jettison or improve). Seek to deepen your involvement in culture through becoming more thoughtful, by reading and studying, by developing your skills, or by talking with others. Treat every aspect of culture as an investment to be developed for the glory of God and the advance of his kingdom (Matt. 25:14–30). Study the Bible for what it has to say about culture matters; read a book by a Christian artist or businessperson; study the works of a past master; take up a new interest, hobby, or craft as a means of expressing your love for God in cultural form. Infuse your involvement with culture matters with prayer and meditation, seeking the Lord and the progress of his kingdom with every gift of culture entrusted to your care and use. From time to time, review your involvement in culture matters to discover what you have learned, or to praise God for the ways your involvement has been consciously improved for the sake of his kingdom.

Develop a plan for fuller, richer engagement in culture matters

Determine that your involvement in culture matters for the sake of the kingdom of God is going to be a lifelong project, and begin setting some goals for yourself: subjects to study, places to visit, uses of culture to acquire or improve, things to learn and to enjoy. Learn to "number your days" (Ps. 90:12) with respect to growing in culture matters, lest the time of your life be taken up by the business of daily existence rather than the sowing, cultivating, and reaping that can produce a rich and satisfying kingdom lifestyle. Plan some time every week for reading, study, contemplation, or discussion of culture matters. Make it a goal to become part of a discussion group concerning culture matters. Search for websites, such as BreakPoint (www.breakpoint.org), My Paruchia (www.myparuchia.com), the Trinity Forum (www.ttf.org), and others, where culture matters are regularly discussed. Take out a subscription to *First Things* or another journal engaging the discussion of culture matters. Determine that, as far as you are able, you are going to spend the rest of your life fulfilling the Lord's plan that you should bring every aspect of your life—all your cultural interests and activities, all your relationships, roles, responsibilities, attitudes, affections, and endeavors—under the headship of King Jesus to be used for his purposes in advancing his realm (Eph. 1:3–14), and set yourself daily to the task of renewing and making progress in that lifelong endeavor.

Involve others with you in your journey

The pursuit of culture matters for the sake of the kingdom of God is an exhilarating and highly enjoyable undertaking. Why do it alone? Some of my most rewarding times in ministry have been when pursuing or enjoying with others some involvement in culture matters from a conscientiously Christian perspective. I have taken friends to art museums, participated in reading groups, and joined with business and professional men to discuss articles from secular journals. Susie and I have hosted cultural discussions in our home. I have worked with others to improve my skills in writing and speaking; attended symphonies, plays, and films with a view to discerning the beauty of the Lord in such cultural endeavors and celebrating it with Susie and others; and shared in the joy of making music together with instruments and voices, not as professionals but simply as *amateurs*—lovers of God and of his gifts of culture. The stimulation, insights, affirmation, benefit, and enjoyment I and others find in such activities encourage me to continue seeking ways of bringing all the culture matters of my life to the feet of Jesus for his approval and use.

Guidelines for Responsible Communities

If a genuine consensus on culture matters is to be achieved within the Christian community, individual believers must lead the way; however, we must also seek to involve our churches in this endeavor.

There are things each of us can do to begin helping our churches to take a more active part in achieving the kind of consensus on culture matters I outlined above. It would be difficult to gauge, but not to imagine, the great strength for cultural enrichment and improvement that might be realized in our communities if our churches were to become centers of cultural critique, creation, equipping, and celebration. Surely the reality of the kingdom would begin to break out from behind the walls of our assemblies and make its presence known, with greater beauty and joy, in all the areas of community life (Ps. 48:1–3). At the same time, we might expect to meet with certain opposition on the part of those whose vested interest in depraved or degrading cultural forms might be threatened by the churches' renewed cultural involvement in their communities (Acts 19:23–41; 17:1–9; Eccles. 7:29; Ps. 45:6).

Promote cultural awareness and engagement

The study of culture matters must become more consistently a part of the preaching and teaching ministries of local churches. Pastors and teachers at all levels, as they begin to become more culturally self-conscious and to grow in their own understanding and use of culture, must bring their insights to bear on the work of equipping the saints for ministry. As preaching and teaching begin to touch base more consistently with a wide range of culture matters, individual believers will be encouraged to become more culturally aware and self-consciously engaged in culture matters from the perspective of the kingdom of God. This, in turn, will open the door within their communities for more specific studies in culture matters, and thus help to establish this as a focus in the ongoing training and teaching of the body of Christ.

In addition, churches can give encouragement to those whose gifts and callings find them serving the Lord in the arts. Discussion groups, fairs and exhibits, workshops and seminars, recitals and readings are but a few ways that churches are already using their facilities and resources to promote greater creative activity on the part of their members. Our own church recently sponsored an afternoon festival in the arts, involving scores of church members exhibiting everything from photography to painting to furniture-making. But such church-wide encouragement need not be limited to the arts. Redeemer Presbyterian Church in New York City provides opportunities for business and professional people to join together for mutual encouragement and study in seeking the kingdom of God through their callings in the culture. Many churches provide training for parents, tutoring for students, alternative schooling opportunities, and outlets for cross-cultural ministry in cities and foreign countries. In a church I served in suburban Philadelphia, we held an annual seminar in writing to encourage members of our community to develop their abilities in this field and to seek outlets for serving the Lord and his kingdom. The church paper we produced incorporated many of the students of that seminar in a wide variety of genres.

As church leaders begin to think more seriously and consistently about ways their congregations can influence the shape and direction of culture, they will make a significant contribution toward achieving a Christian consensus on culture matters.

Establish dialogue and collaboration with members of other communities

Then let church members reach out to other congregations, to share their ideas and experiences, and find ways of joining together to seek a kingdom approach to culture matters that involves churches from other communions. Pastors can begin meeting with other pastors, laypeople with their friends, and students with other students to discuss the church's calling in affecting the shape of culture. Members of various churches can create coalitions, begin study or action groups, or sponsor monitoring teams to raise questions about the state of local culture and to call the churches to more responsible involvement. Opportunities might be created, through involvement of members from various congregations, for improving local schools through PTAs and volunteer work; increasing and improving political participation through voter education projects; assisting struggling art galleries and museums; supporting local orchestras or musical societies; or creating greater cultural awareness by sponsoring reading groups in libraries and bookstores. Websites can be created, newsletters distributed, and announcements or reviews published in local media, all in an attempt to promote greater Christian consciousness and consensus in culture matters. But such activities will be most effective when they involve members from various congregations studying, praying, and working together to achieve and express a Christian consensus on culture matters.

*Join with other communions for the advancement
of distinctly Christian cultural forms*

I have known churches in Baltimore and Northern Virginia (they doubtless exist in other places as well) that, while having but limited resources, have sponsored significant arts fairs and celebrations involving local writers, painters, sculptors, musicians, and storytellers. In many places in the country members of various congregations have united to form Christian classical schools, or to sponsor home-schooling networks, complete with competitive teams in various sports. In our community it is not uncommon for two or three churches to work together in bringing a Christian musician to the area for a concert and conversation. What more could be done by churches on behalf of kingdom expressions of culture across the broad spectrum outlined by Niebuhr?

One of the sad legacies of the Protestant Reformation is the taken-for-granted nature of our separateness as congregations. Every church has its membership, facilities, programs, missions, and doctrinal distinctives. We have little interest in what other churches in the community are doing, and no incentive to work together on behalf of larger objectives or more compelling visions. We have allowed everything that could divide us to do so, and we have sought little that might help us come together to demonstrate our oneness in Christ before the watching world.

Uniting for creative engagement in culture matters might be a way of breaking down some of the barriers that divide congregations of the Lord's people, and of creating a greater sense of unity in the body of Christ locally (John 17:21).

*Unite to discover ways of bringing Christian culture to bear
on contemporary life*

Churches are already doing this, at least to some extent. Recently the church I serve held a community-wide seminar on the history of the Bible, complete with visiting scholars, exhibits of ancient manuscripts and facsimiles, and samples of the some of the earliest published Bibles. This was done in conjunction with other churches, local media, and the Knoxville Convention Center and provided a service in the history of Christian culture that our community otherwise might never have known. The involvement of churches in the work of Habitat for Humanity is another example of how a culture of charity and hard work can serve the common weal. In Crossville, Tennessee, on the Cumberland Plateau, members of various churches became concerned about the growing number of "meth orphans"—those children left parentless because of the incarceration of their addicted moms and dads—and created a home for such orphans, which serves as a way station for them until they can be adopted by proper families. Here again the local community receives the benefit of the culture of compassion, sacrifice, and service that Christians working together can demonstrate before the watching world. Christians from churches all over the country continue going to the stricken Gulf Coast to help rebuild the homes and lives of the victims of Hurricane Katrina, impacting an entire region with the kind of cultural commitment that changes lives.

Culture matters span the spectrum of human interest and activity, and a kingdom distinguished by righteousness, peace, and joy in the Holy Spirit will certainly offer an interpretation and approach to culture that must stand out amid and speak prophetically to the chaos and cacophony of contemporary life. The more churches come together to study, work, and demonstrate the beauty and goodness of the culture of the kingdom, the more their presence in the community will be appreciated and their witness to the truth heeded.

A Christian Consensus?

Is it too much to hope that contemporary Christians might find a way beyond "live-and-let-live" to more visible oneness in their approach to culture matters? That remains to be seen. But if we can agree on some common objectives—a sound critique of culture, the creation of distinctly Christian cultural forms, education for kingdom living, an appreciation of our cultural heritage, and a prophetic culture serving both the church and the larger community—then we can begin to consider, as individual believers and responsible communities, what the best steps for each of us to take might be. To continue our present division over culture matters can only be disastrous in the long run, contributing to even greater marginalization of the church from the day-to-day realities of life. On the other hand, the realization of a Christian consensus on culture matters can be a powerful means to furthering a healthy ecumenism, validating the message of the kingdom, and bringing to greater realization its promise of beauty, goodness, and truth for a sinful, hurting world. Surely these are ends worthy of our efforts in behalf of just such a consensus.

Questions for Study or Discussion

1. Do you believe a Christian consensus on culture matters, such as is outlined in this chapter, is a desirable objective? Why or why not? What obstacles are presently keeping you from beginning to contribute to the realization of that consensus?
2. Review the goals you set for yourself at the beginning of this study. Have you made any progress toward realizing these? Have your goals changed? What steps are you taking?
3. Has this study sparked your interest in culture matters in any particular ways? Do you find you are becoming more culturally self-conscious? Do you plan to do any additional study in culture matters as a result of this study?
4. What are some things you might do to begin getting your church more involved in culture matters? Could you talk with the pastor? Create a study group? Something else?
5. Given the trajectory of American culture over the past two generations—during which time the division of the Christian community over culture matters has continued unchecked—what do you think lies ahead for the next generation of Christians, if we in our generation fail to work for a Christian consensus on culture matters? Will American culture improve or continue to decline? Will the churches become more relevant to cultural life—and to social and moral issues—or will they continue to slide further to the margins of society? If you could do only one thing to change this situation, what would it be?

Notes

1. Culture Watch

1. Unless otherwise indicated, all scripture quotations are from The Holy Bible, English Standard Version, copyright© 2001 by Crossway Bibles, a division of Good News Publishers. Used by permission. All rights reserved.

2. For more on the need for and legitimacy of such criticism, see my *Redeeming Pop Culture: A Kingdom Approach* (Phillipsburg, NJ: P & R, 2003), 79ff.

3. Henry Chadwick, *The Early Church* (London: Penguin Books, 1993), 225.

4. Certainly the apologists of the second century, as well as Tertullian in the third and the desert fathers of the third and fourth centuries, must be considered as having offered important critiques of the culture of their day. None of their work, however, was as sweeping, powerful, or widely read as *City of God*.

5. *City of God* is not, in the first instance, a work of cultural criticism. It may be regarded as a work of Christian philosophy (cf. David Knowles, *The Evolution of Medieval Thought* [New York: Random House, 1962], 37–38), Christian historiography (cf. Christopher Dawson, "Christianity in a Barbarian World," in *Religion and World History: A Selection from the Works of Christopher Dawson*, ed. James Oliver and Christina Scott, [Garden City, NY: Doubleday, 1975], 178), or, more traditionally, as a work of Christian apologetics. However, because much of Augustine's evaluation of the claims of his opponents required extensive analysis of the history and culture of Rome, we should expect to discover in him aspects of an approach to the critique of culture that can be useful for us as well. As Henry Chadwick observes, "*The City of God* moves from a criticism of pagan religion and philosophy to an evaluation of government and society" (Chadwick, *Early Church*, 226).

6. Saint Augustine, *The City of God*, trans. John Healey (London: Dent, 1967), I.III, Vol. 1, 5.

7. Major sections of Book II are involved in responding to this claim.

8. *City of God*, II.XIX, vol. 1, 59.

9. What follows should not be regarded as a thorough examination of any of the aspects of Augustine's critique of Roman culture. My intention is merely to sample those aspects, illustrating by examples from *City of God* an approach to the criticism of culture that can serve us well in our day.

10. John J. O'Meara, ed., *An Augustine Reader: Selections from the Writings of Augustine* (Garden City, NY: Doubleday, 1973), 314.

11. Augustine, *City of God*, I.VIII, vol. 1, 10.

12. Ibid., 11.

13. Ibid.

14. Ibid., I.XV, vol. 1, 20.

15. Ibid., I.VIII, vol. 1, 11.

16. Ibid., IV.I, vol. 1, 112.

17. Ibid., VI.I, vol. 1, 178.

18. Ibid., I.I, vol. 1, 2.

19. Ibid., II.II, vol. 1, 41.

20. Ibid., II.XIX, vol. 1, 59.

21. Ibid., II.VIII, vol. 1, 47.

22. Ibid., II.IV, vol. 1, 43.

23. Ibid., II.XIII, vol. 1, 51.

24. Ibid., II.XXV, vol. 1, 70.

25. Ibid., III.XXXI, vol. 1, 110.

26. Ibid., II.VI, vol. 1, 45.

27. Ibid.

28. Ibid., II.XIX, vol. 1, 59.

29. As, for example, when he appealed to Varro, one of the most respected philosophers of the day, to show that the best thinkers in Rome considered the gods to have been mere human inventions, ibid., VI.III/IV, vol. 1, 182–83.

30. Knowles, *Evolution of Medieval Thought*, 37.

31. Augustine, *City of God*, IV.XXXI, vol. 1, 140.

32. Ibid., VI.II, vol. 1, 180–81.

33. Ibid., VIII.V/VI, vol. 1, 229–30.

34. Ibid., VIII.IX, vol. 1, 233.

35. Ibid., X.I, vol. 1, 273.

36. Ibid., XXII.XXIV, vol. 2, 393.

37. Ibid., 394–95.

38. Sir Ernest Barker, "Introduction," *City of God*, ix.

39. Many of the barbarian tribes flooding the Roman Empire in the late fourth century had come under the influence of the gospel, albeit in the form of Arianism, under the preaching of Ulfilas (311–381), who also translated part of the Bible into the Gothic language.

40. He would make precisely this argument in Book V.

41. Augustine, *City of God*, I.I, vol. 1, 2.

42. Ibid., I.XXXII, vol. 1, 37.

43. Ibid., II.XXIX, vol. 1, 75.

44. Ibid., II.XIII, vol. 1, 51–52.

45. Ibid., V.I, vol. 1, 143.

46. Ibid., V.II–VI, vol. 1, 144ff.

47. Ibid., V.VII, vol. 1, 149.

48. Ibid., I.III, vol. 1, 4. The gods of Rome were believed to be fugitive gods of Troy, destroyed by the Greeks.
49. Ibid., II.XXI, vol. 1, 63.
50. Ibid., III.XX, vol. 1, 101.
51. Ibid., IV.XI, vol. 1, 123.
52. Ibid., III.XVII, vol. 1, 94–95.
53. Barker, "Introduction," xi, xii.
54. Augustine, *City of God*, IX.V, vol. 1, 265.
55. Ibid., IX.XVII, vol. 1, 268.
56. Ibid., X.VI, vol. 1, 279.
57. Ibid., X.XXXII, vol. 1, 309.
58. Ibid., XXI.XXVI, vol. 2, 350.
59. Barker, "Introduction," viii.
60. Augustine, *City of God*, XIX.IV, vol. 2, 237.
61. Ibid., 238.
62. Ibid., XIX.V, VI, vol. 2, 241–42.
63. Ibid., XIX.X, vol. 2, 245–46.
64. Ibid., XIX.XIV, XV, vol. 2, 251–53.
65. Ibid., XIX.XVII-XX, vol. 2, 254–57.
66. Ibid., XIX.XXI-XXVI, vol. 2, 259–65.
67. Ibid., XIX.XXVII, vol. 2, 266.
68. Ibid., XXII.XXX, vol. 2, 408.
69. Cf. Ezek. 33:1–9 and Eph. 5:15–17. See also Cornelius Van Til's description of the apologist as one stationed on the wall of God's city, *Christian Apologetics*, ed. William Edgar (Phillipsburg, NJ: P & R, 2003), 22–23.
70. *Re:Generation Quarterly* ceased publication in 2003, but the archives can be found at www.ctlibrary.com/rq/.
71. For a sample copy or subscription, email to subscriberservices@pma-inc.net, or write to *First Things*, 156 Fifth Avenue, Suite 400, New York, New York 10010.

Chapter 2. Forging New Culture

1. Evidence for this renewed interest is of many different kinds, including popular histories such as Thomas Cahill, *How the Irish Saved Civilization* (New York: Doubleday, 1995); Peter Berresford Ellis, *Celtic Inheritance* (New York: Dorset Press, 1992); Jean Markale, *The Celts* (Rochester, VT: Inner Traditions International, 1993); reprints of such standbys in the field as J. Romilly Allen, *Celtic Art* (London: Senate, 1904, 1997); Nora Chadwick, *The Celts* (London: Penguin Books, 1971, 1991); and Charles Plummer, ed. and tr., *Lives of Irish Saints*, vols. 1 and 2 (Oxford: Clarendon Press, 1922, 1997); popular anthologies such as Christopher Bamford and William Parker Marsh, *Celtic Christianity: Ecology and Holiness* (Great Barrington, MA: Lindisfarne Press, 1987); Anthony Duncan, *The Elements of Celtic Christianity* (Rockport, MA: Element, 1992); Kenneth Hurlstone Jackson, ed. and tr., *A Celtic Miscellany* (London: Penguin Books, 1971); and Robert Van de Meyer, ed., *Celtic Fire* (New York: Doubleday, 1990); other popular literature, including manuals of spirituality such as Oliver Davies and Fiona Bowie, *Celtic Christian Spirituality* (New York: Continuum, 1995); and Shirley Toulson, *The Celtic Year* (Shaftesbury: Element Books Limited, 1993); first-person accounts, such as James Charles Roy, *Islands of Storm* (Chester Springs, PA: Dufour

Editions, 1991); and such period novels as Geoffrey Moorhouse, *Sun Dancing* (New York: Harcourt Brace, 1997). There is also a growing body of scholarly literature on various aspects of this period, including Lisa M. Bittel, *Isle of the Saints* (Ithaca, NY: Cornell University Press, 1990); Catherine E. Karkov, Robert T. Farrell, and Michael Ryan, eds., *The Insular Tradition* (Albany: State University of New York Press, 1997); Mary Low, *Celtic Christianity and Nature* (Edinburgh: Edinburgh University Press, 1997); James P. Mackey, *An Introduction to Celtic Christianity* (Edinburgh: T & T Clark, 1989); John Marsden, *The Fury of the Northmen* (London: Kylie Cathie, 1996); Liam De Paor, *St. Patrick's World* (Notre Dame, IN: University of Notre Dame Press, 1993); Philip Sheldrake, *Living between Worlds: Place and Journey in Celtic Spirituality* (Boston: Cowley Publications, 1995); and E. A Thompson, *Who Was St. Patrick?* (New York: St. Martin's Press, 1985). Of course, numerous works specifically devoted to Celtic art, and Celtic Christian art in particular, are also available. These include Janet Backhouse, *The Lindisfarne Gospels* (London: Phaidon Press, 1993); Derek Bryce, *The Symbolism of the Celtic Cross* (York Beach, ME: Samuel Weiser, 1995); Miranda Green, *Celtic Art: Symbols and Imagery* (New York: Sterling, 1996); Peter Harbison, *The Golden Age of Irish Art* (London: Thames and Hudson, 1999); Lloyd and Jennifer Laing, *Art of the Celts* (London: Thames and Hudson, 1992); Bernard Meehan, *The Book of Kells* (London: Thames and Hudson, 1994); Ruth and Vincent Megaw, *Celtic Art: From Its Beginnings to the Book of Kells* (London: Thames and Hudson, 1991); Barry Raftery, ed., *Celtic Art* (Paris: UNESCO and Flammarion, 1996); and Jakob Streit, *Sun and Cross* (Edinburgh: Floris Books, 1984). A series of books explaining various aspects of Celtic Christian art for contemporary artists is available from Thames and Hudson Publishers (New York). There is even a growing number of recordings of Celtic spiritual music, including *Bards and Ballads: Ancient Celtic Music* (London: Topic Records, 1995); *The Brendan Voyage* (Dublin: Tara Record Co., 1980); Eden's Bridge, *Celtic Psalms* (Brentwood, TN: StraightWay Music, 1997); Eden's Bridge, *Celtic Worship* (Brentwood, TN: StraightWay Music, 1997); *Celtic Spirit* (Milwaukee: Narada Media, 1996); Aine Minogue, *The Mysts of Time* (East Greenwich, RI: North Star Music, 1996); Noirin Ni Riain, *Soundings* (Boulder, CO: Sounds True, 1993); Noirin Ni Riain, *Vox de Nube* (Boulder, CO: Sounds True, 1992). It is also interesting to see the growing selection of Celtic Christian jewelry and other period-inspired artifacts in various mail order catalogs.

2. Robert Wilken, *Remembering the Christian Past* (Grand Rapids: Eerdmans, 1995), 180.

3. Illustrations and helpful explanations of specific examples of Celtic Christian art can be found at the Celtic Art Forms website, www.joellessacredgrove.com/Celtic/art. html and at Book of Kells Images, www.snake.net/people/paul/kells. An online search reveals hundreds of such sites.

4. Hilary Richardson, "Celtic Art," in Mackey, *Introduction to Celtic Christianity,* 367; Green, *Celtic Art,* 161, 162. Cf. the comment by Allen that follows.

5. Karkov, Farrell, and Ryan, *Insular Tradition,* 63.

6. Green, *Celtic Art,* 167.

7. Allen, *Celtic Art,* 254.

8. Celtic Christian artists were not ones to waste surface space, whether vellum, metal, or stone. There is little in a page of an illuminated manuscript or on the arms of a stone cross that is not crowded with jostling or interlaced figures of one sort or another.

9. Green, *Celtic Art,* 167.

10. Allen, *Celtic Art*, 242; Backhouse, *Lindisfarne Gospels*, 47; Green, *Celtic Art*, 51, 155–56; Megaw and Megaw, *Celtic Art*, 11.

11. Michael Ryan, "Aftermath: Celtic Christianity," in Raftery, and Megaw, *Celtic Art*, 130.

12. Allen, *Celtic Art*, 13, 38, 43; Megaw, 21.

13. Allen, ibid., 253.

14. Bryce, *Symbolism of the Celtic Cross*, 128. Cf. Allen, ibid., 169–71; Green, *Celtic Art*, 36, 51; Karkov, Farrell, and Ryan, *Insular Tradition*, 91; Laing, *Art of the Celts*, 115; and Streit, *Sun and Cross*, 111–12.

15. Megaw and Megaw, *Celtic Art*, 20, 253.

16. Streit, *Sun and Cross*, 149.

17. Cf. Laing, *Art of the Celts*, 146–48.

18. Bryce, *Symbolism of the Celtic Cross*, 54, 60, 68; Green, *Celtic Art*, 156; Streit, *Sun and Cross*, 124–54.

19. Richardson, in Mackey, 373.

20. Karkov, Farrell, and Ryan, *Insular Tradition*, 79ff; cf. the dramatic photograph in Raftery, and Megaw, *Celtic Art*, 126–27.

21. Sheldrake, *Living between Worlds*, 49.

22. Backhouse, *Lindisfarne Gospels*, 22.

23. Green, *Celtic Art*, 51.

24. Allen, *Celtic Art*, 253.

25. Arthur C. Danto, *Art After the End of Art* (Princeton, NJ: Princeton University Press, 1997), 41ff.

26. Cf. the argument concerning early Christian art in Paul Corby Finney, *The Invisible God* (Oxford: Oxford University Press, 1994).

27. Cf. David Levi Strauss, "Rescuing Art from Modern Oblivion," *Wilson Quarterly*, Summer 1997.

28. Cf. Marci Whitney-Schenk, "Abstract Art," *Christianity and the Arts*, Summer 1998.

29. Cf. Harbison, *Golden Age*, 56, 68.

30. The full interview with Phil Keaggy appeared in my column *Ars Poetica*, on BreakPoint.org, summer 2001.

3. Education for Cultural Renewal

1. See C. John Miller, *Outgrowing the Ingrown Church* (Grand Rapids: Zondervan, 1986), 27ff; cf. Howard A. Snyder with Daniel V. Runyon, *Decoding the Church* (Grand Rapids: Baker, 2002), 37ff.

2. Robert E. Webber, *Ancient-Future Faith* (Grand Rapids: Baker, 2000), 145.

3. Craig Dykstra, *Growing in the Life of Faith* (Louisville: Geneva Press, 1999), 67.

4. Ibid., 78.

5. An earlier version of this chapter, "Some Observations concerning the Educational Philosophy of John Calvin," appeared in *Westminster Theological Journal* 46, no. 1 (Spring 1984), 140ff.

6. W. Stanford Reid, "Calvin and the Founding of the Academy of Geneva," in *Westminster Theological Journal* 18, no. 1 (November 1955), 2.

7. John Calvin, *Institutes of the Christian Religion* (Grand Rapids: Eerdmans, 1953), 4.8.8.

8. Ibid., 1.10.2.

9. Henry Beveridge and Jules Bonnet, *Selected Works of John Calvin: Tracts and Letters*, trans. David Constable (Grand Rapids: Baker, 1983), 7 vols., vol. 5, *Letters, Part 2, 1545–1553*, 279.

10. *Ecclesiastical Ordinances, 1541* in Philip E. Hughes, *The Register of the Company of Pastors of Geneva in the Time of Calvin* (Grand Rapids: Eerdmans, 1966), 35.

11. Ronald S. Wallace, *Calvin, Geneva, and the Reformation* (Grand Rapids: Baker, 1988), 113.

12. Ibid., 106.

13. Reid, "Calvin and the Founding," 8.

14. *Ecclesiastical Ordinances*, 40–41.

15. Calvin, *Institutes*, 1.5.

16. Reid, "Calvin and the Founding," 22.

17. Wallace, *Calvin, Geneva, and the Reformation*, 125.

18. Calvin, *Institutes*, 4.1.5.

19. Cf. ibid., 1.17.6, 4.1.1.

20. "Articles concerning the Organization of the Church and of Worship at Geneva, 1537" in J. K. S. Reid, ed., *Calvin: Theological Treatises* (Philadelphia: Westminster, 1954), 54.

21. Ibid., 49.

22. Calvin, *Institutes*, 4.1.1–4.

23. The Geneva Confession, in Reid, *Theological Treatises*, 32.

24. *Ecclesiastical Ordinances*, 40.

25. Ibid., 40–41.

26. Ibid. For more detail on the curriculum of the formal schools in Calvin's Geneva, see Elmer L. Towns, "John Calvin (1509–1564)" in *A History of Religious Educators*, ed. Elmer Towns (Grand Rapids: Baker, 1975), 169–72.

27. See the many minutes concerning the review of preaching and teaching in Hughes, *Register of the Company of Pastors*.

28. Calvin, *Institutes*, 2.2.12.

29. Ibid., 1.5.1.

30. Ibid., 1.5.2.

31. Ibid., 1.5.9.

32. Ibid., 1.7.4.

33. Ibid., 1.2.1.

34. Ibid.

35. Ibid.

36. Ibid.

37. Ibid., 1.5.10.

38. Ibid., 1.2.1.

39. Ibid., 1.1.1

40. Ibid., 2.1.3.

41. Ibid., 1.15.3.

42. Ibid., 1.15.17.

43. Ibid.

44. Ibid., 1.3.3.

Notes

169

45. John Calvin, *Commentaries on the Catholic Epistles* (Grand Rapids: Eerdmans, 1959), 200.
46. Calvin, *Institutes*, 4.1.5.
47. Genevan Confession, 32.
48. *Ecclesiastical Ordinances*, 47.
49. Ibid.
50. Catechism of the Church of Geneva, in Reid, *Theological Treatises*, 130.
51. Calvin, *Institutes*, 4.1.5.
52. Ibid.
53. Catechism of the Church of Geneva, 130.
54. Calvin, *Institutes*, 1.4.2.
55. Ibid., 4.1.5.
56. Cf. Reid, "Calvin and the Founding," 23ff.
57. *Ecclesiastical Ordinances*, 47.
58. Reid, "Calvin and the Founding," 23ff.
59. E. William Monter, *Calvin's Geneva* (Huntington: Robert E. Krieger, 1975), 108.
60. Robert D. Knudsen, "Calvinism as a Cultural Force," in W. Stanford Reid, ed., *John Calvin: His Influence in the Western World* (Grand Rapids: Zondervan, 1982), 28–29.

4. Foundations for a Christian Cultural Consensus

1. I have elaborated this point somewhat more extensively in my four-part series Contend for the Faith, in my column *Second Sight*, on BreakPoint.org (see archives).
2. Cf. Thomas C. Oden, *The Rebirth of Orthodoxy: Signs of New Life in Christianity* (New York: HarperCollins, 2003), and Robert E. Webber, *Ancient-Future Faith: Rethinking Evangelicalism for a Postmodern World* (Grand Rapids: Baker, 1999).
3. From this point, the remarks that follow—minus the interview with Chuck Colson—appeared, in a somewhat more condensed form, in *Reformation & Revival Journal* 14, no. 4 (2005).
4. Concerning Kuyper as an example, Bolt writes, "his example of combining orthodox, evangelical, Calvinistic piety with explicitly religious social and political activism has become an attractive and inspiring model for North American Christians (Bolt, *A Free Church, A Holy Nation: Abraham Kuyper's American Public Theology* [Grand Rapids: Eerdmans, 2001], xiii).
5. See L. Praamsma's excellent summary of these various positions in *Let Christ Be King: Reflections on the Life and Times of Abraham Kuyper* (Jordan Station, Ont.: Paideia Press, 1985).
6. In addition to Praamsma's little book, see also John Bolt, *Free Church;* McKendree R. Langley, *The Practice of Political Spirituality* (Jordan Station, Ont.: Paideia Press, 1984); and Frank Vanden Berg, *Abraham Kuyper* (St. Catherine's, Ont.: Paideia Press, 1978). What follows is summarized primarily from these works.
7. Abraham Kuyper, *Lectures on Calvinism* (Grand Rapids: Eerdmans, 1983), 11.

8. Abraham Kuyper, "Uniformity: The Curse of Modern Life," in *Abraham Kuyper: A Centennial Reader*, ed. John D. Bratt (Grand Rapids: Eerdmans, 1998), 19ff.

9. Abraham Kuyper, "The Blurring of the Boundaries," in Bratt, *Abraham Kuyper*, 396.

10. Ibid., 401.

11. Abraham Kuyper, "Sphere Sovereignty," in Bratt, *Abraham Kuyper*, 467.

12. Ibid., 467–68.

13. These notions are well summarized in Abraham Kuyper, "Common Grace in Science," in Bratt, *Abraham Kuyper*, 441ff.

14. Kuyper, "Sphere Sovereignty," 488.

15. Kuyper, "Common Grace in Science," 456.

16. See especially his *The Practice of Godliness* (Grand Rapids: Baker, 1977).

17. Ibid., 458.

18. Kuyper, *Lectures on Calvinism*, 107.

19. Kuyper, "Maranatha," in Bratt, *Abraham Kuyper*, 219–20.

20. Kuyper, *Lectures on Calvinism*, 30.

21. See his discussion on the image of God in "Common Grace in Science," 445.

22. Kuyper, "Maranatha," 212.

23. Kuyper, "Common Grace in Science," 447.

24. Kuyper, *Practice of Godliness*, 29.

25. Ibid., 30.

26. Ibid., 116–17.

27. Abraham Kuyper, *Sacred Theology* (Wilmington, DE: Associated Publishers and Authors, n.d.), 19, 250.

28. Kuyper, *Lectures on Calvinism*, 143.

29. Ibid., 166–67.

30. Kuyper, *Practice of Godliness*, 42; "Maranatha," 214; *Lectures on Calvinism*, 82–83.

31. Kuyper, "Common Grace in Science," 458.

32. Information on "Wide Angle," the Colson/Warren conversations about biblical worldview for use with small groups, can be found on BreakPoint.org.

5. The Prophetic Power of Culture

1. An earlier form of the following remarks, minus the section on David Wilcox, appeared as "A Prophet in the Wasteland: The Christian Legacy of Czeslaw Milosz," in *Theology Today* 62, no. 2 (July 2005). Used by permission.

2. Czeslaw Milosz, "*Ars Poetica?*" in *The Collected Poems* (Hopewell, NJ: Ecco Press, 1988), 211.

3. Cf. Eric Ormsby, "Of Lapdogs & Loners: American Poetry Today," in *The New Criterion*, April 2004, 6.

4. Joy Sawyer, *Dancing to the Heartbeat of Redemption* (Downers Grove, IL: InterVarsity Press, 2000), 28. Cf. also Brad Leithauser's remarks to the effect that "free verse at the moment shows signs of exhaustion" in *The Formalist* 10, no. 1 (1999), 51ff.

5. Dana Gioia, *Can Poetry Matter? Essays on Poetry and American Culture* (St. Paul: Graywolf Press, 1992), 1–14.

6. Robert Faggen, ed., *Striving towards Being: The Letters of Thomas Merton and Czeslaw Milosz* (New York: Farrar, Strauss and Giroux, 1997), 63.

7. In Czeslaw Milosz, *Provinces: Poems 1987–1991*, Czeslaw Milosz and Robert Haas, tr. (Hopewell, NJ: Ecco Press, 1991), 1.

8. Czeslaw Milosz, "Prayer," in his *New and Collected Poems, 1931–2001* (New York: Ecco Press, 2003), 743.

9. Czeslaw Milosz, *The Witness of Poetry* (Cambridge: Harvard University Press, 1983), 23ff.

10. Czeslaw Milosz, *The Captive Mind* (New York: Vintage Books, 1990).

11. Faggen, *Striving towards Being*, 11, 118.

12. Ibid., 30–31.

13. Czeslaw Milosz, *Roadside Dog* (New York: Farrar, Strauss and Giroux, 1998), 77.

14. In Czeslaw Milosz, *Facing the River*, trans. Czeslaw Milosz and Robert Haas (Hopewell, NJ: Ecco Press, 1995), 10.

15. Milosz, *New and Collected Poems, 1931–2001*, 742.

16. In Milosz, *Collected Poems*, 235.

17. Milosz, *Witness of Poetry*, 27, 37, 49, 66.

18. In Milosz, *Collected Poems*, 111.

19. Ibid., 212.

20. Faggen, *Striving towards Being*, 89.

21. In Milosz, *Collected Poems*, 222.

22. Dietrich Bonhoeffer, *Life Together*, trans. John W. Doberstein (San Francisco: Harper and Row, 1954), 29.

23. Faggen, *Striving towards Being*, 118.

24. Milosz, *Provinces*, 32.

25. Karl Shapiro, "What Is Not Poetry," in Reginald Gibbons, ed., *The Poet's Work: 29 Poets on the Origins and Practice of Their Art* (Chicago: University of Chicago Press, 1989), 106.

26. Milosz, *Witness of Poetry*, 73–74.

27. In Milosz, *Collected Poems*, 49.

28. Milosz, *Roadside Dog*, 138–39.

29. In Milosz, *Collected Poems*, 258. This poem serves as the frontispiece for *The Witness of Poetry*.

30. Milosz, *Roadside Dog*, 71.

31. Milosz, *Facing the River*, 31.

32. In Milosz, *Collected Poems*, 324.

33. Milosz, *New and Collected Poems*, 634.

34. Michael Polanyi, *Science, Faith, and Society* (Chicago: University of Chicago Press, 1964), 81.

35. Natalie Goldberg, *Writing Down the Bones* (Boston and London: Shambhala, 1986), 99.

36. T. M. Moore, *Consider the Lilies: A Plea for Creational Theology* (Phillipsburg, NJ: P & R, 2005).

37. Milosz, *Witness of Poetry*, 115.

38. An earlier, expanded form of the following appeared in my column *Ars Poetica*, on BreakPoint.org.

6. Toward a Christian Consensus

1. H. Richard Niebuhr, *Christ and Culture* (New York: Harper & Row, 1951, 1975), 231.

2. Ibid., 32–33.

3. Ibid., 256.

4. Paul Johnson, *Creators* (New York: HarperCollins, 2006), 1–5.

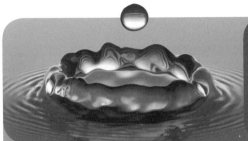

Brazos Press is grounded in the ancient, ecumenical Christian tradition, understood as living and dynamic. As legend has it, Brazos is the Spanish name explorers gave to a prominent Texas river upon seeing how its winding waters sustained fertile soil in an arid land. They christened this life-giving channel Los Brazos de Dios, "the arms of God."

Our logo connotes a river with multiple currents all flowing in the same direction, just as the major streams of the Christian tradition are various but all surging from and to the same God. The logo's three "streams" also reflect the Trinitarian God who lives and gives life at the heart of all true Christian faith.

Our books are marketed and distributed intensively and broadly through the American Booksellers Association and the Christian Booksellers networks and bookstores; national chains and independent bookstores; Catholic and mainline bookstores; and library and international markets. We are a division of Baker Publishing Group.

Brazos Book Club and Border Crossings

Brazos books help people grapple with the important issues of the day and make Christian sense of pervasive issues in the church, academy, and contemporary world. Our authors engage such topics as spirituality, the arts, the economy, popular culture, theology, biblical studies, the social sciences, and more. At both the popular and academic levels, we publish books by evangelical, Roman Catholic, Protestant mainline, and Eastern Orthodox authors.

If you'd like to join the Brazos Book Club and receive our books upon publication at book club prices, please sign up online at **www.brazospress.com/brazosbookclub**.

To sign up for our monthly email newsletter, Border Crossings, visit **www.brazospress.com**. This email newsletter provides information on upcoming and recently released books, conferences we are attending, and more.

BrazosPress
The Tradition Alive